PRAISE FOR PRINCE

"Regardless of how long Prince had known or ~~worked~~ with any of his studio staff, "stardom has ~~never interfere~~ e work, and there was never a mo~~ment~~ ld pull rockstar on you."

"Perhaps more than any other artist, Prince called the tune for pop music in the Eighties, imprinting his Minneapolis sound on an entire generation of musicians both black and white."
—Rolling Stone Magazine

"Prince designed Purple Rain as the project that would make him a superstar, and...that is exactly what happened."
—Billboard Magazine

"On 'Parade,' especially, Prince was testing new musical territory—and now, moving like an inchworm, he's letting his tail catch up with his head. Dance grooves and all, 'Sign o' the Times' reaffirms Prince's ambitions while reasserting his popularity."
—New York Times'

"(Graffiti Bridge) is Highly Recommended "...purely and unabashedly tuneful...a sultry, groovy inventively jittery jewel box of diverse nuggets."
—Spin Magazine

PRINCE
'in the Studio'
1975-1995

by Jake Brown

PRINCE
'in the Studio'
1975-1995

by Jake Brown

COLOSSUS BOOKS

PHOENIX   NEW YORK
LOS ANGELES

PRINCE 'in the Studio' 1975-1995
by Jake Brown

Published by:
Colossus Books
A Division of Amber Communications Group, Inc.
1334 East Chandler Boulevard, Suite 5-D67
Phoenix, AZ 85048
Amberbk@aol.com
WWW.AMBERBOOKS.COM

Tony Rose, Publisher/Editorial Director
Yvonne Rose, Associate Publisher
The Printed Page, Interior Design / Cover Layout

COLOSSUS BOOKS are available at special discounts for bulk purchases, sales promotions, fund raising or educational purposes.

"PRINCE 'in the Studio' 1975-1995"

ISBN#: 978-0-9790976-6-9

Library of Congress Cataloging-in-Publication Data

Brown, Jake.
  Prince in the studio : 1975-1995 / by Jake Brown.
    p. cm.
  Includes bibliographical references and index.
  ISBN 978-0-9790976-6-9 (alk. paper)
1. Prince. 2. Rock musicians--United States--Biography. I. Title.

ML420.P974B76 2010
781.66092--dc22
[B]

2010041506

Acknowledgments

First and foremost, I would like to thank my longtime publisher, Amber Communications Group, Inc., specifically owners Tony and Yvonne Rose, for supporting the release of this book, which I've wanted to write for years. The fact that it marks my 20th published book is especially important to me on a professional level; and that that mark is passed with another book from my 'In the Studio' series focused on my greatest musical influence, Prince, makes it even more personally touching for me.

Next, of course, I want to dearly thank the producers and engineers who contributed their time and memories to assisting the reconstruction of the recording of this majestic catalog of beautiful music, thank you for your contributions both to that legacy, and to this book's study of it, specifically Susan Rogers, David Leonard, Michael Koppelman, Sylvia Massey, Ross Pallone, Steve Fontano, Chuck Zwicky, and an EXTRA SPECIAL THANK YOU to Eddie Miller for your interviews/pics.

Equally, I want to give MANY THANKS to Matt 'Dr' Fink for devoting the extensive lengths of time you did to fleshing out the aforementioned catalog from a band member's intimate perspective, I was a big fan, and am an even bigger one now, thank you for your help bringing this book to life

I would also like to cite the following research sources: princetext. tripod.com/ 'Prince in Print'; www.prince.org, www.housequake.com; *'Dancemusicsexromance : Prince—The First Decade'* by Per Nilsen; *'Purple Reign: The Artist Formerly Known As Prince'*—by Liz Jones; and *'Possessed: The Rise and Fall of Prince'* by Alex Hahn

Personal Thank Yous: to my wonderful parents, James and Christina Brown, my brother Sgt. Joshua 'Jerry' Brown (RET!!!), congrats on Triple Crown! Alex, Lindsay and Jackson Schuchard; Andrew and Sarah McDermott; Chris Ellauri (Ongking.com!); Sean and Amy Fillinich; Richard, Lisa and Regan Kendrick; Paul and Helen; Adam 'The Skipper' Perri; Matt and Eileen Pietz, congrats on the little one; Tim Woolsey; Penelope Ellis; Reed Gibbons; Ed Seamen, Rachel, Dave, Larry, Burt Goldstein and everyone else at MVD/Big Daddy Music Distribution who keep Versailles Records' product out there in stores; Harry Slash; Jack David, David, Crissy, Simon, and everyone else at ECW Press who have supported the advancement of my writing career with your publication of 'Heart: in the Studio, (Authorized)' 'Rick Rubin: in the Studio,' and forthcoming 'Tori Amos: in the Studio'; Lemmy Kilmister for collaborating with me on 'Motorhead: in the Studio' (Fall, 09); Kurt and Cris Kirkwood for 'Meat Puppets: in the Studio' (2010!); and Jasmin St. Claire/Rhea, can't wait for the book to be out—it's been a blast!!

Contents

Introduction:

'Purple Genius—The Revolution of Prince'

Originating his very own funk-pop musical genre that produced over 100 million albums sold world-wide; six Grammy Awards among tens of dozens of award nominations over the past 30 years; induction into the Rock & Roll Hall of Fame in 2004 and a world-tour the same year which grossed $87 million—making it the #1 most profitable tour of the year, Prince proved he was as relevant in the millennium as he'd been since the late 1970s when he first introduced what *Rolling Stone Magazine* describes in sound and impact as a "taut, keyboard-domi-nated...hybrid of rock, pop, and funk, with blatantly sexual lyrics...(that) influenced much of 1980s dance-pop music...Madonna...Michael... and Janet Jackson were comparable to Prince only in terms of star power. None could match the formidable breadth of his talents, which included not just singing and dancing but also composing, producing, and playing instruments."

Taking the foundational fusion of funk and new wave that predecessors like Stevie Wonder, Sly and the Family Stone and Rick James had first introduced to the pop mainstream to its next musical level, Prince invented a new style of music that the record making/buying world simply hadn't been acquainted with prior thereto. This was so much the case that *Rolling Stone Magazine* further concluded that while "James Brown may have been the hardest-working man in show business, but no one in the history of rock & roll has covered more ground than Prince... Anyone partial to great creators should own (his records)... Like Jimi and Sly, Prince is an original; but apart from that, he's like no one else." Channeling another worldly musical talent that has inarguably gone unmatched in the entire history of Rock & Roll, Prince's self-taught command of 31 musical instruments inspired Rock & Roll's biggest magazine to more broadly credit Prince as "the most influential record producer and arranger of the '80s." The Philadelphia Enquirer, for its own part, has concluded that "Prince earned his reputation by taking songs that were already a cut above ordinary and transforming them into invigorating, provocative statements. Even before his 1984 breakthrough with Purple Rain, his albums predicted trends in pop the way Davis' did in jazz. His deft use of dissonance, symphonic orchestration, polytonality and jarringly syncopated rhythms instantly separated him from everyone else on the charts."

Longtime engineer Eddie Miller, in offering his own eye-witness assessment of Prince's influence, further reasoned that "Prince is such a great culmination of music history to this point in time. It's as if he took all the best of the great ideas of the last century, and figured out a way to put it all together. And as if that weren't enough, he mastered the art of performance on top of all this. The thing I really admired was that I realized it didn't just happen. Prince essentially gave his life to get to this level, and that's the definition of a musical hero." Others who have worked closest with Prince don't pretend to begin to fully understand the depths of his talent, with Revolution keyboardist Lisa Coleman for one, pointing as a reason why to the fact that "his mind is out there, not just on another planet, it's in another galaxy" while longtime engineer Chuck Zwicky explained that "Prince has such a deep connection with melody, harmony, and rhythm, and an unbelievable ability to express and communicate it. I can't really think of anyone you could compare him to—maybe Stevie Wonder."

In the pages of '*Prince 'in the Studio*' that sum is broken down into the individual parts, i.e. albums—a staggering 27 albums over the past 3 decades—that compose Prince's living legend. Focusing on his most prolific, popular and prized—among fans—recording period, spanning 1975-1995, '*Prince: In the Studio*' reveals the prodigal childhood roots of Prince's genius growing up in working-class inner-city Minneapolis in multiple homes. Finding his refuge in an even greater number of instruments, Prince signed to Warner Bros. Records, while still a teen-ager. Becoming the first newly-signed artist in the label's history to produce his own debut LP—simply because no other producer could have translated his musical genius to tape as authentically.

Over the next 10 years, Prince would reinvent the sonic boundaries of pop music, in a flurry of 13 albums in 13 years that *Billboard Magazine* summarized to include highlights such as "1980's *Dirty Mind*. He recorded his first masterpiece, a one-man tour de force of sex and music; it was hard funk, catchy Beatlesque melodies, sweet soul ballads, and rocking guitar pop, all at once. The follow-up, *Controversy*, was more of the same, but *1999* was brilliant. The album was a monster hit, sell-ing over three million copies, but it was nothing compared to 1984's *Purple Rain*. Purple Rain made Prince a superstar; it eventually sold over ten million copies in the U.S. and spent 24 weeks at number one… In 1986, he released the even stranger *Parade*, which was in its own way as ambitious and intricate as any art rock of the '60s; however, no art rock was ever grounded with a hit as brilliant as the spare funk of '*Kiss*.' By 1987 Prince's ambitions were growing by leaps and bounds, resulting in the sprawling masterpiece *Sign 'O' the Times*."

By the late 1980s, Prince had become such a powerhouse that he attracted fellow living legends like Miles Davis and George Clinton to his WEA-distributed Paisley Park label, where in his own right, he continued to churn out stylistically ground-breaking classics, includ-ing 1988's legendary bootleg LP '*Black Album*', which *Rolling Stone* praised for its "James Brown horn licks, assorted grunts and groans… (and) guitar leads that burned into your skull", and its commercial replacement studio release, '*LoveSexy*', which *Rolling Stone* also hailed in its 4-Star review as "complex…as the black album was locomotive and sexual…(revealing) how intricate and complex Prince's concept of funk has grown since 1980's *Dirty Mind*." Heading into the 1990's with the hugely popular Motion Picture Soundtracks to *'Batman'* and *'Graffiti Bridge'* respectively, producing hits like *'Batdance'* and *'Thieves in the Temple,'* Prince was tiding fans over for his next pop tidal wave, which came in 1991 with the release of the 12x platinum *'Diamonds and Pearls,'* with which *Billboard Magazine* pointed out he "skillfully reinvented himself as an urban soulman without sacrificing his musical innovation." Within the first half of that decade, he would also release two other hit albums under the 'Prince' moniker with 1992's *'LoveSymbol'* LP, and 1994's *'The Gold Experience.'* Now, for the first time, in the pages of *'Prince: in the Studio—1975-1995'*, we will explore the first two decades and fifteen studio albums of a legacy that seems to be ever-expanding as the Millennium—and Prince's prolific studio catalog—do in the same time…

"John Nelson, leader of the Prince Rogers jazz trio, knew Mattie Shaw from North Side community dances. A singer sixteen years John's junior, Mattie bore traces of Billie Holiday in her pipes and more than a trace of Indian and Caucasian in her blood. She joined the Prince Rogers trio, sang for a few years around town, married John Nelson and dropped out of the group. She nicknamed her husband after the band; the son who came in 1958 got the nickname on his birth certificate. At home and on the street, the kid was 'Skipper.' "

—*Rolling Stone Magazine*

Chapter 1:

Prince 'Skipper' Roger Nelson—1958-1968

One of Rock & Roll's greatest stars—Prince Roger Nelson—was born to father John T. Nelson, (who was bi-racial) and mother Mattie Shaw (who was Italian) on June 7th, 1958 at Mount Sinai Hospital in Minneapolis, Minnesota, with Prince's mother Mattie recalling that her first child from the union, whom she nicknamed 'Skipper', "was so small in size and he was just real cute, he was a darling baby." Prince's father, meanwhile, explained that "I named my son Prince because I wanted him to do everything I wanted to do." John Nelson's grand ambitions for his son stemmed in part from his day job as a Plastic Moulder at the Honeywell

5

Electronics plant by day, while working as a struggling musician by night, having met Prince's mother—Mattie Shaw—while singing back-up in his jazz band. Much to both his parents' delight, during the future superstar's early childhood, his gift for music was obvious, so much so that Prince's mother Mattie recalled that "he could hear music even from a very early age…When he was three or four, we'd go to the department store and he'd jump on the piano, the organ, any kind of instrument there was. Mostly the piano and organ. And I'd have to hunt for him, and that's where he'd be, in the music department." Prince's father John further recalled that "when he was five, he would play the piano…He would copy me, but he could also do things I couldn't do."

Prince's only sibling, Tika 'Tyka' Evene, was born 2 years later in 1960, to John and Mattie, joining an extended family of siblings from his parents' previous marriages—including two half-sisters Lorna and Sharon and half-brother John Jr. his father's prior relationships, as well as a half-brother Alfred, from previous relationship. Recalling just how unusual a duo Prince and sister Tyka were during their formative years, Tyka recalled that it began with the fact that "my name was very different, and with Prince at the school as well, we got teased about our names all the time. I mean, back in the 60s, no one was called Tyka and Prince." Prince's musical ambitions grew in real time with his own development as a musical prodigy, coupled with his discovery of the live component of performance, which the future superstar recalled began when his father John T. Nelson took him along to his live gigs, with Prince recalling years later that "it was great, I couldn't believe it, people were screaming. From then on, I think I wanted to be a musician."

Prince's ability to connect with his father via their shared love of music was key to any closeness the pair shared during Prince's younger years, mainly because outside of that realm of musical commonality, the musician explained years later that "my mom's the wild side of me; she's like that all the time. My dad's real serene; it takes the music to get him going. My father and me, we're one and the same…It's real hard for my father to show emotion…He never says, 'I love you,' and when we hug or something, we bang our heads together like in some Charlie Chaplin movie. But a while ago, he was telling me how I always had to be careful.

My father told me, 'If anything happens to you, I'm gone.' All I thought at first was that it was a real nice thing to say. But then I thought about it for a while and realized something. That was my father's way of saying 'I love you.' " For his own part, John Nelson explained that much of his introversion grew out of the fact that " I spend a lot of time by myself, writing and composing music. That's the most important thing to me. I don't care to meet strangers. I express myself through my music and my son does too. That's how we communicate our feelings. A lot of his talent comes from God, maybe some from me."

Prince's musical evolution was further encouraged during his grade-school years attending John Hay Elementary School when he befriended Andre 'Cymone' Anderson, who would become his best friend and musical sidekick for the remainder of their adolescence. Upon meeting and realizing their fathers had once played in the same band, Prince's father on piano and Andre's on bass, Andre recalled that "I couldn't believe it, because Prince and I immediately got on so well, and here we had something else in common. It was deep." Little did Prince know it at the time, but not only would his friendship with Andre be key to his musical development as the years went on, it would also provide a solid foundation for him domestically as his own had begun to crumble, such that by his 7th birthday, his parents had divorced. In a *Rolling Stone Magazine* profile years later, the publication reported that "John Nelson moved out of the family home when Prince was seven. But he left behind his piano, and it became the first instrument Prince learned to play. The songs he practiced were TV themes—*Batman* and *The Man From U.N.C.L.E.* 'My first drum set was a box full of newspapers,' he has said, explaining how he came to play a whole range of instruments."

"The product of a broken home,
Prince found refuge in music."
—Rock & Roll Hall of Fame

Chapter 2:

Broken Home, Broken Hearts—1969-1972

Leaving Mattie, Prince and Tyka to live in the house on 915 Logan Avenue in Northern Minneapolis, the impact of father John T. Nelson's departure upon Prince was enormous, with sister Tyka recalling that "I can vividly remember the day my father left…I just stood in the front room with this little guy and I looked up at him and said 'Now what?'" Elaborating on the personal fall-out post-Prince's father leaving the family, Prince's sister further recalled that to support her two children, newly-single mother Mattie was forced to work the kind of long hours that sadly left them latchkey kids, such that, as Tyka recalled, "I was brought up by Prince and the television…I quite often think I'm a character from Little House on the Prairie. And neither of us can watch it without bursting into tears. Prince taught me everything I know. We grew up spending a lot of time on our own. That made us creative. He taught me how to draw and write stories. When my mother and father divorced, he was the only person living in the house with me, so he took on the father role. My mother was working three jobs, keeping everything together." Elaborating on the affects his family's sudden financial instability had on him, Prince later recalled that "we used to go to…McDonald's (and)…I didn't have any money, so I'd just stand outside there and smell stuff. Poverty makes people angry, brings out their worst side. I was very bitter when I was young. I was insecure and I'd attack anybody." Prince's sister Tyka further observed that as a result of the combination of responsibility and instability placed on him in the same time, "(Prince) was forced to grow up too soon…So in some ways he never did at all."

Not surprisingly, Prince filled the absence of his father with a musical therapy that the superstar years later explained was a catalyst of sorts to "communicate what I was feeling. I spent a lot of time alone and I turned to music. I played all the time. The music sort of filled a void." The promise of domestic normalcy returned briefly to Prince's world when his mother remarried his stepfather, Haywood Baker, who Prince recalled took him to a James Brown concert as a sort of bonding experience, such that "when I was about 10 years old, my step-dad (took me to a James Brown concert and)…put me on stage with him, and I danced a little bit until the bodyguard took me off. The reason I liked James Brown so much is that, on my way out, I saw some of the finest dancing girls I had ever seen in my life. And I think, in that respect, he influenced me by his control over his group."

Sadly, for Prince, once his father John left home, it seemed permanently broken, such that the singer recalled the summary impact as one wherein "I ran away from home when I was twelve…I've changed my address in Minneapolis thirty-two times, and there was a great deal of loneliness…I was constantly running from family to family. It was nice on one hand, because I had a new family, but I didn't like being shuffled around. I was bitter for a while, but I adjusted." *Rolling Stone Magazine* further substantiated this reality years later in a cover story when it reported that once "Mattie and John broke up…Prince began his domestic shuttle." For a brief time during this period, Prince was reunited with his father when he went to live with John T. Nelson and his new family. Attending Bryant Junior High School with best friend Andre as well as some of his step-siblings, Prince initially had a rough reception, such that he recalled years later that "I went through a lot when I was a boy...They called me sissy, punk, freak and faggot. See, the girls loved you, but the boys hated you." Half-sister Lorna, who also attended Bryant Junior High, recalled that her brother was "always bullied...Every day the bigger kids would wait for him. He dreaded walking up those steps. They used to jeer him because he was so short and had a black-Italian background. What really hurt him were the taunts he used to get at basketball practice."

Things weren't much easier during this time for Prince at home with his father, who threw him out after catching his son home alone with a girlfriend after school one day. Describing the fallout that followed, Prince recalled that "I called my dad and begged him to take me back after he kicked me out...He said 'no', so I called my sister and asked her to ask him. So she did, and afterward told me that all I had to do was call him back, tell him I was sorry, and he'd take me back. So I did, and he still said 'no'. I sat crying at that phone booth for two hours. That's the last time I cried." For Prince, being bounced around so constantly had only one silver living, and not surprisingly, it was a musical one, wherein after "I went to live with my aunt, she didn't have room for a piano, so my father bought me an electric guitar, and I learned how to play."

After a bit more of the domestic musical chairs, Prince was taken in by his best friend Andre's family, a move that would prove to be a key catalyst to the birth of what *Rolling Stone Magazine*, years later, would deem "the first notes of the Minneapolis sound... heard in a big brick house in North Minneapolis, an aging, primarily black section of town that draws outsiders only to the Terrace Theater, a movie house designed to look like a suburban backyard patio, and the Riverview Supper Club, the nightspot a black act turns to after it has polished its performance on the local chittlin circuit. North Minneapolis is a poor area by local standards, but a family with not too much money can still afford the rent on a whole house. It was there that Bernadette Anderson, who was already raising six kids of her own by herself; decided to take in a doe-eyed kid named Prince, a pal of her youngest son, Andre. The thirteen-year-old Prince had landed on the Anderson doorstep after having been passed from his stepfather's and mother's home to his dad's apartment to his aunt's house."

The transition proved a calming one for Prince in the context of establishing a sense of domestic stability. Still Bernadette Anderson recalled that generally during that period in his life, due to all he'd been through, Prince "never said much, but he was an emotional volcano that could erupt at any moment. The fury showed itself when school friends teased him about his height. They were very cruel." Best friend Andre Cymone further recalled that "he came and lived with us and I think actually my mother adopted him and he lived with our family for a while." Elaborating on the latter, Prince explained years later that "I took a lot of heat all the time (in school)...People would say something about our clothes or the way we looked or who we were with, and we'd end up fighting. I was a very good fighter...I never lost. I don't know if I fight fair, but I go for it." Prince would live with the Andersons for the duration of his teenage years, with 2nd cousin/future bandmate Charles recalling that Andre's mother, Bernadette, became the closest thing Prince had thereafter to an authority figure, describing her as "an absolutely amazing part of his life...She was mom to everybody. You didn't get out of line. You helped with the chores. As soon as the car came with all the groceries, she shared everything with everybody." Bandmate and best friend Andre Cymone remembered feeling that Prince "dug the atmosphere. It was freedom for him."

After setting up a bedroom/rehearsal space in Bernadette's basement, Prince and Andre formed their first band together, with Prince handling guitar/piano, Andre bass, and Cousin Charles drums. Initially called Phoenix before being changed to Grand Central, which bandmate Andre Cymone recalled was "something I think Prince came up with 'cause he was really into Grand Funk Railroad." Prince's drummer/cousin Charles recalled that at first the band "tried to imitate the Jackson 5. Prince was singing 'I Want You Back'...(and at first) we thought it was a girl singing that. The Jackson 5 was a big inspiration because they were our age and we thought we could beat them. We said 'We're just as talented, and we've got the same kind of vibe and everything...(Prince) was more into Sly Stone and heavier stuff. Stevie Wonder was Prince's main person; he loved Stevie's work, but he said 'Man, I could do that!' And the same with Sly, except for the fact that he knew Sly was always blasted, and missing his concerts and stuff. Prince would go, 'I'm not going to be like Sly, I'm going to practice my behind off like James Brown's band, and I'm going to have everything so tight that you're not going to be able to say anything about it.' We were always very competitive." Andre Cymone added that "we rehearsed in my mom's basement and we got a chance to develop and learn through that whole situation." Reciting some of the musical influences he brought to Grand Central, Prince recalled "Carlos Santana, Jimi Hendrix, and James Brown, of course. On piano, I was influenced by my father, who was influenced by Duke Ellington and Thelonius Monk. I like to say I took from the best."

Recalling that once Grand Central got started, they never truly stopped playing. Bernadette Anderson explained that "they'd play all the time… Sometimes it'd drive me crazy. I'd be in bed, and everyone's supposed to be sleeping, and all of a sudden I'd hear this guitar in the basement, and Prince was playing Minnie Ripperton, and singing it. Sometimes I'd go holler, and other times I'd just let him go ahead. Then above my head was Andre doing the same thing… It sounded like a lot of noise, but after the first couple of years I realized the seriousness of it. Girls were crazy about them". Elaborating, Andre Cymone recalled that "the thing about my situation is that my mother was going through an interesting period in her time herself, so she gave us a lot of freedom. Not only was Prince there at my house but Morris and a lot of other people. Some other friends came and you know how in the neighborhood there's always one house that everybody kind of comes to and hangs out at? That was my crib…Everybody came to my crib 'cause we could rehearse there and my mom was totally cool. She wasn't trying to sweat us about making the noise, she wasn't sweating us about having girlfriends, you know, even when we were 14, 15 years old. So she was cool, so we had fun."

"Prince was a real smart kid, he could do a lot of things in 10 minutes that took some people a whole hour to do."

—Gene Anderson
(former Social Studies teacher)

Chapter 3:

Central High School—1972-1973

By the time Prince and Andre were nearing the end of junior high school, Grand Central had added Andre's sister Linda Anderson to the group on keyboards, as well as Terry Jackson and William Doughty on percussion. As the group became more accomplished and serious about their musical development, drummer Charles recalled that "Andre's basement had all these centipedes and spiderwebs, and it was always flooded. Our equipment was always in danger of getting wet...We eventually moved over to neighbor/percussionist Terry Jackson's basement, because he lived next door, and said 'Come over to our house and practice instead.' So we ended up rehearsing there. In fact, we went back and forth between Terry and Andre's basement." Using the refuge of Bernadette's basement to develop as a lead guitarist, both during rehearsals with Grand Central and in between on his own during a period of almost constant practice.

Prince developed a unique style of playing wherein he explained that "I tuned it to a straight A, so it was really strange. When I first started playing guitar, I just did chords and things like that, and I didn't really get into soloing and all that til later."

At 14, Prince began attending 9th grade at the ethnically-diverse inner-city Central High School, explaining years later in how it shaped him that "I grew up on the borderline...I had a bunch of white friends, and I had a bunch of black friends. I never grew up in any one particular culture...I was very lucky to be born here because I saw both sides of the racial issue, the oppression and the equality. I got the best of all worlds here, I saw what happens here, and it's not like what happens in, say, Atlanta." Elaborating on how that exposure would inform his music years later, Prince in hindsight recalled that "I was brought up in a black-and-white world and, yes, black and white, night and day, rich and poor. I listened to all kinds of music when I was young, and when I was younger, I always said that one day I would play all kinds of music and not be judged for the color of my skin but the quality of my work, and hopefully I will continue. There are a lot of people out there that understand this, 'cause they support me and my habits, and I support them and theirs."

Not surprisingly, in school Prince centered his attention squarely on music, explaining that his focus began because "my older brother (Duane) was the basketball star...He always had girls around him. I think I must have been on a jealous trip, because I got out of sports." Naturally, thereafter, he had another talent to fall back on, one which high school music instructor, Jim Hamilton, recalled Prince had in common with the 100% he'd given to basketball before choosing to focus full-time on music because of "his work ethic...(which was) one of his greatest qualities...If he wanted to accomplish something, he would really work at it. If there was something he was going to practice, he would sit there for an hour or two hours, and he would not stop until it had been accomplished." Amazingly, Prince's intense focus on his musical studies weren't at the expense of any others during this period, with his former Social Studies teacher Gene Anderson, for one example, recalling that "Prince was a real smart kid, he could do a lot of things in 10 minutes that took some people a whole hour to do." The bottom line: for Prince, there was nothing academically—or personally—more important to him during this period than his musical pursuits, such that the superstar would admit years later that during high school, "(I) missed out on a lot, but I don't regret it. I missed out on socializing. But I got high off playing my music or going to a movie alone."

Soon after beginning at Central High School, Prince and Andre befriended classmate Morris Day, who soon thereafter joined Grand Central at Prince's invitation, replacing Cousin Charles on the drums. Morris, for his part, recalled the evolution of his life-long musical/personal relationship with Prince as one that began when the pair "hooked up back in high school. Of course, he went to Central, which was south Minneapolis, and I went to North, which was obviously north Minneapolis. But we both lived in north Minneapolis. I hooked up with Andre Cymone. We both went to North, started hanging out together, and he told me about his band, man, and I went to see these guys play, which (Prince)'s cousin at the time, Charles Smith, was on drums. And the band was incredible. These guys were like 14 years old, man. They were playing like they were 25. You know, guitar solos, Andre was plucking on the bass. It was just incredible. And I just became, like, a fan of their band, which was called Grand Central at the time, and, you know, Andre and I started hanging out. He came over to my house one day. We were cutting class. *Kids, don't do that. I don't recommend it.* But we was cutting class, and he came over to my house, man, and, you know, we found out—I told him I played drums. But he heard me play. He was, like, 'Man, you're good.' You know, he's, like, 'We just happened to be having some scheduling problems with our current drummer.' So that's when I went and auditioned for them a few days later, and that was it, man. I got the gig, man, and then, you know, Prince was sort of a real standoffish character, you know. He sort of talked through Andre to me for the first couple of weeks, and then after that, we started having direct conversations, and then we became real tight. But that's basically it—We were about 14, 15 years old at that time."

Amid the musical influences shaping him via Grand Central, Prince's musical pallet was also informed by radio stations including KUXL, the city's only 'black' station, as well as progressive rock station KQRS, with Prince recalling that "it was about 6 months late for things to get (to Minneapolis,) but...after midnight, that was the bomb station. I'd stay up all night listening to it. That's where I discovered Carlos Santana, Maria Muldaur, and Joni Mitchell. Was I influenced by that? Sure I was. Back then I always tried to play like Carlos or Bob Scaggs...(So) James Brown played a big influence in my style...Another big influence was Joni Mitchell. She taught me a lot about color and sound, and to her, I'm very grateful." Still, at the time, Prince seemed willing to admit that he hadn't quite matured to the aforementioned level as a lyricist, such that "When I got into high school, I started to write lyrics. I'd write the really, really vulgar stuff."

"As Prince and his band, Grand Central, continued to expand in popularity throughout Minneapolis' electric live club circuit, the band often traveled to local hotels and gyms to band-battle with their black competition: Cohesion, from the derided 'bourgeois' South Side, and Flyte Time, which, with the addition of Morris Day (years later after the disbandment of Grand Central), would later evolve into the Time."

—Rolling Stone Magazine

Chapter 4:

Grand Central Corporation—1974-1975

From Grand Central's vantage point, bassist Andre Cymone recalled that "the interesting thing is, it wasn't scary at all for us. I mean the cool thing about us, I think 'cause we had a little four-piece band at the time, so playing and performing was something that was in everybody's blood. I know it was in mine and I know it was in Prince's. Morris wasn't in the band at the time but my sister was in the band. It was kind of a very small situation... we had a battle of the bands. It's interesting, 'cause at the time they were much older than we were and at the time they had all this really, really nice equipment. Just big amplifiers, nice guitars, they had a horn section and they had this guitar player that was rich so he had like a wah-wah pedal and all this other kind of cool stuff. We didn't have nothing! It was just me, Prince, a drummer, and a percussionist, you know, and everybody laughed at us when we came up and thought that we were gonna lose and all that kind of stuff. You know, we had all this really bad equipment, it didn't have any paint on it. So we went up to them, 'You guys, can we like play on your stuff, man? You know, we promise we ain't gonna break it.' So it was like, 'Yeah, yeah go ahead.' It was like letting the little kids, yeah let them go ahead. Man we turned it out! People came back. People were leaving and they came back and we won the battle of the bands and we played the rest of the night."

Boasting a live repertoire that featured covers by such heyday rock, psychedelic pop, R&B and funk superstars as Sly and the Family Stone; Jimi Hendrix; James Brown; Earth, Wind and Fire; Parliament; the Four Tops; and Stevie Wonder, Grand Central was fast becoming one of Minneapolis' hottest up and coming buzz bands. Recalling how the covers his band included in their live set influenced the original compositions he wrote for the band, Prince explained that because "we basically got all the new music and dances three months late...I just decided that I was gonna do my own thing. Otherwise, when we did split Minneapolis, we were gonna be way behind and dated. The white radio stations were mostly country, and the one black radio station was really boring to me. For that matter, I didn't really have a record player when I was growing up, and I never got a chance to check out Hendrix and the rest of them because they were dead by the time I was really getting serious. I didn't even start playing guitar until 1974."

Recalling the band's live heyday, Prince's sister Tyka remembered that "we used to go to talent shows and street parades at a place called United Way on the north side of the city. It was painted red, black, and green, and had a black power attitude. They used to block off the streets and the bands would play. Prince also played to tourists and businessmen." In spite of his and his father's hot-cold relationship, Prince's talent had won over John T. Nelson as one of his # 1 fans, with cousin/former bandmate Charles recalling of Nelson's attendance of son's shows that "I remember him being there most of the time...with his camera, taking

pictures…He was intense about it too, taking pictures from all angles."
In describing the social fabric of the underground new wave club scene
his band was helping to shape, Prince explained that 'Uptown,' the
strip where First Avenue and other popular live rock clubs populated,
was "pretty different. Uh, kinda sad, to be exact. I mean, the radio was
dead, the discos was dead, ladies was kinda dead, so I felt like, if we
wanted to make some noise, and I wanted to turn anything out…I was
gonna have to get somethin' together….which is what we did. We put
together a few bands and turned it into Uptown." As further detailed in
later years by *Rolling Stone Magazine*, "the 'Uptown' Minneapolis scene
was starting to generate heat and included rival bands like Flyte Time
(consisting of Jimmy Jam, Terry Lewis, Jellybean Johnson, Monte Moir
and vocalist Cynthia Johnson) and The Family. Unrelated to Prince's
future side project of the same name, The Family was bassist Sonny
Thompson's group, and Prince and Cymone would jam with him at his
home, improving their techniques. The local scene was largely impro-
vised; Linda Anderson recalls, "We just made our own gigs. We would
go around and just play in neighborhoods, set up our equipment in the
park and play, and have people gather 'round." Longtime local radio
personality Walter 'Q-Bear' Banks, head programmer at KMOJ-FM,
recalled that in the mid-1970s, "it was more of a family-knit thing back
then…Flyte Tyme, Grand Central, they were brothers that I grew up
with. We played football on Saturday mornings over at Lincoln Field
right off of Penn. Parents brung us Kool-Aid." Though they positioned
themselves as musical competitors on the live scene, Prince's admiration
for the group's collective—and individual—musical talents were clear
with his comment years later, following the group's split, that "Jesse
and Morris and Jerome and Jimmy and Terry had the makings of one
of the greatest R&B bands in history. I could be a little pretentious in
saying that, but it's truly the way I feel. There's no one that could wreck
a house like they could. I was a bit troubled by their demise, but…it's
important that one's happy first and foremost."

"1976—Central High Pioneer School
Newspaper Interview:

Nelson Finds It "Hard To Become Known"

'I play with Grand Central Corporation. I've been playing with them for two years,' Prince Nelson, senior at Central, said. Prince started playing piano at age seven and guitar when he got out of eighth grade. Prince was born in Minneapolis. When asked, he said, 'I was born here, unfortunately.' Why? 'I think it is very hard for a band to make it in this state, even if they're good. Mainly, because there aren't any big record companies or studios in this state. I really feel that if we would have lived in Los Angeles or New York or some other big city, we would have gotten over by now.' He likes Central a great deal, because his music teachers let him work on his own. He now is working with Mr. Bickham, a music teacher at Central, but has been working with Mrs. Doepkes. He plays several instruments, such as guitar, bass, all keyboards, and drums. He also sings sometimes, which he picked up recently. He played saxophone in seventh grade but gave it up. He regrets he did. He quit playing sax when school ended one summer. He never had time to practice sax anymore when he went back to school. He does not play in the school band. Why? 'I really don't have time to make the concerts.' Prince has a brother that goes to Central whose name is Duane Nelson, who is more athletically enthusiastic. He plays on the basketball team and played on the football team. Duane is also a senior. Prince plays by ear. 'I've had about two lessons, but they didn't help much. I think you'll always be able to do what your ear tells you, so just think how great you'd be with lessons also,' he said. 'I advise anyone who wants to learn guitar to get a teacher unless they are very musically inclined. One should learn all their scales too. That is very important,' he continued. Prince would also like to say that his band is in the process of recording an album containing songs they have composed. It should be released during the early part of the summer. 'Eventually I would like to go to college and start lessons again when I'm much older.' "

With a growing ambition on display and clearly focused beyond the Twin Cities, Grand Central drummer Morris Day recalled that bandmates "Prince and Andre were so serious minded. That was all they talked about, 'When we make it...' 'When we get our deal, we'll become famous.'" Prince proved particularly astute at quickly sizing up and down the droves of 'managers' and 'booking agents' who hounded him after Grand Central shows promising the stars, but chose instead to go with an extended member of the inner family in LaVonne Daughtery, mother of drummer Morris Day, who in turn hooked the group up with local music producer Pepe Willie, who had already become a familiar source of music advice to Prince via his marriage to one of Prince's cousins, Shauntel Manderville.

As a relative and fan of Prince in the same time, Willie recalled that "LaVonne wanted somebody who was in the music industry, someone who knew what to do with (Grand Central)... I was introduced to Prince in 1974 by my fiancée', Prince's cousin, Shauntel. She was excited about Prince because he was a very talented musician. She knew I really knew about the business of music and she wanted me to talk to Prince. He was playing at a ski party in Minnesota when we met. I remember thinking, 'Boy, he's got a big Afro.'...I considered Prince (to be) family, so I wanted to tell him everything I possibly knew. They had some great ideas but their material wasn't constructed properly. They would just start playing and singing, and then they would jam for 15 minutes. Everybody was playing together, that wasn't the problem. The problem was they weren't singing together. I told them to put down their instruments."

Elaborating further, Pepe Willie recalled that, not surprisingly, "Prince was the most talented guitar player, and I would have him play the chords and get them to all sing together... Of course, there was raw talent there, but when they began to sing, everyone was singing something different. Prince was singing 'she', André was singing 'he', the rest of the group was singing something else; and the name of the song was *You Remind Me of Me* (written by André). I couldn't believe they didn't take the time as a group to learn the words. So I had them put down their instruments and start learning the lyrics. You know, it was like Song Construction 101 had begun. Of course, my No. 1 student was

Prince…I taught them about song construction, singing together, the best ways to rehearse together, but I didn't have to tell Prince anything more than once. "

Clearly seeing something uniquely special in Prince, Willie offered the already accomplished musician and now-aspiring recording engineer the opportunity to work as studio session player for his 94 East recording sessions at Cookhouse Studios in December, 1975, which would become Prince's first known studio recording. Comprised of a band that included older Minneapolis session staples such as Dale Alexander on drums, Wendell Thomas on bass, back-up singers Kristie Lazenberry and Marcy Ingvoldstad, Pierre Lewis on keyboards, Prince on lead guitar alongside Lewis on guitar and lead vocals. The group's first session produced five recordings, including 'If We Don't,' 'Better Than You Think,' 'Games,' 'I'll Always Love You,' and 'If You See Me.' Willie recalled of the recording session that Prince "was dependable, eager to please, and inspiring in his performance. Late at night, after a session, I remember, Prince would call me up to tell me that he…was unhappy with something he'd recorded and wanted to redo his tracks. I trusted Prince enough to let him go into the studio by himself and redo the track(s). I mean, that's how talented he was at 16."

From the experience, Prince immediately took Andre and Morris and entered another Minneapolis studio, ASI Studio, a 16-track whole in the wall on the city's North side, which engineer David Rivkin (a.k.a. David Z), who also engineered the session—his first with Prince of many to follow—recalled was a "just a horrible piece of junk" to lay down some demos for his own group. Newly re-named Grand Central Corporation at the urging of group manager LaVonne Daughtery—who was also bankrolling the sessions— Prince produced the demo as well as handling lead vocals, lead guitar and keyboards, while Andre and Morris Day handled bass and drums respectively over the course of demos including *'Lady Pleasure,' 'Machine,' '39ᵗʰ St. Party,' 'You're Such a Fox,' 'Whenever,'* and *'Grand Central.'* These demos would mark the beginning of Prince's years in the studio…

"Prince would normally show up a bit earlier than everybody else, thrash around on the drums a little bit, twinkle on the piano, bass, guitar or whatever..."

—Chris Moon (Moonsound Studios)

Chapter 5:

From Champagne to the Moon (Sound Studios)—Spring, 1976

Once Prince and company had recorded their first demos with Prince handling the majority of the tracks' instrumentation and production, his mind appeared to have opened beyond the studio to the full range of possibilities he could infuse into his live act, such that Grand Central Corporation evolved into Champagne, with Prince recalling that after "I got my first band (Grand Central)...I wanted to hear more instruments, so I started Champagne, a twelve-piece band. Only four of us played. Eight were faking. Andre and I played saxophone. I also played piano. I wrote all the music. The songs were all instrumentals. No one ever sang." Bandmate Andre Cymone further recalled that "think right around that time Prince had split, he had gotten a solo deal with Warner Brothers. So he split and we just changed the name. We actually changed the name before he split but, you know, it wound up being Champagne when he was out of the band."

The group soon dissolved, as Prince focused more and more on advancing his studio craft, with his next big break coming in the late Spring of 1976 upon entering an 8-track studio, Moonsound Studios, nearby Lake Nokomis outside downtown Minneapolis, to record another round of demos with Andre Cymone and Morris Day as the only hold-overs from his previous bands. Describing his initial impression of Prince and company, studio owner Chris Moon recalled that the group was "energetic youngsters…They seemed pretty fun-loving, clean in terms of women, pretty easy-going, happy. There seemed to be a bond amongst them." Singling Prince out from the group, Moon noted that as the sessions progressed, "Prince would normally show up a bit earlier than everybody else, thrash around on the drums a little bit, twinkle on the piano, bass, guitar or whatever…Prince always used to show up at the studio with a chocolate shake in his hand, sipping out of a straw…He looked pretty tame. Then he'd pick up an instrument and that was it. It was all over."

Clearly impressed with Prince's multi-instrumental studio prowess, Moon soon took him aside to offer a business proposition that would be Prince's first real education in studio recording, with Moon recalling that "I pulled (him) aside at the end of one session, 'I've got an idea for you. I'm looking for someone to put together some music for some words that I've written…I'm looking to find an artist and provide him with studio time for free, to collaborate on some material. It's a very simple thing, I don't want any contracts, no paperwork, just a handshake. I will develop you as an artist. I will build a package around you, and I will try to get you out there." Prince, seeming to feel it was an opportunity he couldn't refuse, Moon further recalled that "Prince thought about it for a couple of moments, grunted in a positive way, which I believed was a general agreement…We shook hands." In an acknowledgement of just how much trust he was placing in Prince's talent, Moon has later reflected in hindsight that at the time, "it was a pretty bold move on my part. This was a 17-year-old kid from the North Side of Minneapolis, whom I really didn't know. I just handed over the key to everything I own."

In addition to trusting Prince with the keys to his studio, Moon also gave him a crash-course on the operation of his console and related recording equipment, and settled into a routine thereafter where at day's end he would leave Prince with different sets of lyrics he'd written for the artist to come up with musical accompaniments to. For Prince, the deal with Moon essentially ended Champagne, who'd given him an ultimatum upon learning of Moon's proposal of him or them. Years later, Prince would explain his side of the decision to break the group up, recalling that "I asked them all what they wanted to do. 'Do you want to stay here, or do you want to go to New York?' No one wanted to do it. They liked their lifestyle, I guess. I don't think they really liked the idea of my trying to manipulate the band so much. I was always trying to get us to do something different. It was always me against them." Adding context, Andre's mother Bernadete Anderson also recalled that Prince seemed ready to move on from under the management wing of Morris Day's mother, LaVonne Daughtery, explaining that "She wasn't fast enough for Prince...He wanted her to get them a contract right away." Once Prince had taken up recording residency at Moonsound Studios, owner Chris Moon recalled a routine wherein "he'd stay the weekend, sleep on the studio floor...I wrote down directions on how to operate the equipment, so he'd just follow the little chart—you know, press this button to record and this button to play back. That's when he learned to operate studio equipment. Pretty soon, I could sit back and do the listening."

In terms of the music, the pair were collaborating on the creation of in the course of their deal, Moon recalled that "I would either leave new lyrics on the piano for him, or he was already working on something...I was throwing all kinds of stuff out, trying to find something he liked. Interestingly enough, he gravitated more to the lyrics that were non-conventional. Initially, no lyrics flowed from him, but after awhile, he started seeing the rhythm and the rhyme of my lyrics and the approach I was taking. The first ones came pretty difficult for him. He was more musically inclined than words (at first)."

That same spring of 1976, Prince had accrued enough credits to graduate early from Central High School, allowing him to spend all of his time at Moonsound, such that his studio recording skills by this point, as owner Chris Moon recalled, were so advanced that it made Prince akin to "an octopus, because there were hands all over the place." For his own part, Prince recalled that once his time was —quite literally—100% free to devote to developing his own sound, "that's when I really started writing. I was writing like three or four songs a day. I didn't have any school, and I didn't have any dependants, I didn't have any kids, or girlfriends, or anything. I cut myself off from everything." While his father seemed to approve completely of Prince's pursuit of a career as a professional recording artist, he recalled that initially his mother Mattie "wanted me to go to school, go to college. She sent me to a bunch of different schools. I always had a pretty high academic level, I guess. She always tried to send me to the best schools, but that was pretty much my second interest."

"He was the kind of guy who could sit in a room with you and absorb everything in your brain and know more than you by the time you left the room...."

—Owen Husney

Chapter 6:

Leaving for New York— 1976/1977

By the summer of 1976 Prince had accrued enough produced material for a professional demo to shop to major labels, which had been his ultimate intention all along. Moon recalled that "we wanted to put together an album's worth of material, that's why we did 14 songs...I think the tape represented Prince faithfully. It had some diversity: we did things with flutes, rock guitars, some melodic songs, some funk, etc."

With songs including Prince-penned songs like *'Baby,' 'I'm Yours,' 'Since We've Been Together,'* and the aptly-titled *'Leaving for New York,'* Prince soon thereafter did just that in an effort to shop his demo to major labels. Songs that didn't make the demo included such unreleased tracks as *'Nightingale,' 'Spending My Time,' 'Rock Me Lover,'* and *'Don't You Wanna Ride?',* still Prince and Moon felt he had enough material to warrant the interest of A&R reps. Though Moon passed on managing Prince formally, he offered some unofficial assistance, including agreeing to call some labels on Prince's behalf and convincing him to drop Nelson from his professional name, which the artist agreed with.

Upon leaving Minneapolis to pursue his first shot at the big time, Moon explained that "Prince had been in New York a week (staying with his half-sister Sharon Nelson) when he called me and asked why he hadn't been on any appointments? I said 'I'm having a little trouble (with)... these labels, but I'm working on it.' They would say 'Leave your name and we'll get back to you.' " Next hooking Prince up with Minneapolis advertising agent Owen Husney, who ran The Ad Company, Husney recalls being eager to work with Prince, recalling that "I understood Prince's talent immediately. I wasn't per-se sold on the songs, but I was sold on his ability. There was just no doubt in my mind when Chris told me it was one guy playing all the instruments. My first comment to him was 'Who's the band?' And he said, 'It's not a band. It's one guy playing, singing and doing everything.' And I just said 'You gotta be kidding! I mean, this is ridiculous. Where is he? Let's just get him on the phone now." Convincing Prince to return to Minneapolis to further-hone his demo, Prince recalled that in spite of his initial disappointment, "I went back to Minneapolis and back to Andre's basement. I could deal with the centipedes and poverty better because I knew that I could make it. I'd proven it to myself and that's what really mattered."

Upon meeting Husney in person for the first time, the manager recalled that the pair "got on really well, right from the start...We talked about what he wanted to do with his career." With word out about Prince and other managers reaching out from as far as L.A., Husney got right down to the business of getting Prince set up with the right major label, explaining that "I walked out of my $8 million-a-year business for him... (because) his talent was so great...(We) raised something like $50,000 to get Prince off the ground. He needed attention in order to be presentable to the labels." With the two signing a formal management pact under the umbrella of Husney's new company, American Artists Inc., in December 1976. Husney felt in hindsight the gamble he was taking was well worth it because in Prince he had a true business partner, in that "at 17, he had the vision and astuteness of a 40-year-old…He was the kind of guy who could sit in a room with you and absorb everything in your brain and know more than you by the time you left the room. Prince might hang late, but it was all for music. He wasn't looking to get high with the guys."

"Husney put together an expensive package that included a demo tape of three twelve-minute songs on which Prince sang and played all the instruments…"
—Rolling Stone Magazine

Chapter 7:

1977

Heading into the New Year, Husney booked Prince into a new studio, Sound 80, with David Rivkin again engineering, toward the end of further refining Prince's major label demo. Once the pair had hunkered down in Prince's already-routine 24-hour-lock-out record-a-holic fashion, Rivkin initially recalled that "we tried all kinds of stuff because I didn't know how to record…I was first and foremost a musician. People at Sound 80 would tell us, 'You can't do that!' But we were doing it. We'd overload the board and we'd do things that people who knew electronics wouldn't do." The revised demo included new Prince compositions such as re-recorded '*Baby,*' '*Soft & Wet,*' and '*Make It Though the Storm,*' all featuring heavy Oberheim 4-Voice synthesizer, which Prince would thereafter make a regular feature on many of his early studio albums that followed in the years after.

While Prince was hard at work in the studio, as *Rolling Stone Magazine* would later report, "Husney put together an expensive package that included a demo tape of three twelve-minute songs on which Prince sang and played all the instruments, and he went off to L.A. to make a pitch to the record companies. Three labels—CBS, Warner Bros. and A&M… made offers." Husney recalled his strategy was to create a bidding war between the majors, wherein he first "called Russ (Thyret, V.P. and Dir. of Promotion for WEA, and said) 'Russ, listen, CBS is flying us out for a presentation on this kid that can play all the instruments. He's 17 years of age. Do you want to take a meeting with him?' And he said 'Sure!'… And then I called A&M Records, 'Listen, CBS and Warner are flying us out. Would you like to be part of the presentation?' They were like 'Yeah, well, call us when you get there.' I lied my way in everywhere." Elaborating further on the label shopping process, Husney partner/attorney Gary Levinson recalled that "Prince would come into some of the meetings after interest had been generated and they'd ask him questions…He'd answer very matter-of-factly, yes or no, if he could. If they asked him to elaborate, he'd give three or four words."

Not surprisingly, though the offers were quickly rolling in, Prince's terms were as uncommon as he was a recording artist for the times, beginning with his demand that he retain complete recording autonomy in the studio, which would make him the first new artist in any of the labels' history to produce his debut studio LP. As former manager Owen Husney explained, "not one of the labels wanted him to be his own producer… They felt that he was just a young kid who had to learn." To answer the question of whether Prince could in fact handle production on a major-label release, the most interested label, Warner Bros. Records' Lenny Waronker, then head of A&R and eventually president of the label, according to a report in *Rolling Stone Magazine*, "was impressed enough to allow Prince to act as producer of his debut album. 'I met him when we first signed him…(Producer) Russ and I took him into the studio one day, much to his chagrin. So we said, 'Play the drums,' and he played the drums and put a bass part on, a guitar part. And we just said, 'Yeah, fine, that's good enough.'" Elaborating further on the demo, '*Just As Long As We're Together*,' that sold Prince as a producer to the heads at WEA, which included a panel of producer judges including many of the label's—and industry's—biggest of the time: Ted Tempelman (Van Halen) and Lenny Waronker (Everly Brothers, Doobie Brothers, James Taylor) among others, who Husney joked looking back that Prince "thought we were janitors...They were all walking in and out of there. Prince had no idea who the heck it was." Upon okaying Prince's retaining complete creative control in the studio, Warner Bros.' one condition to the arrangement stipulated there be a seasoned executive producer to keep an eye on Prince during production, which the artist and management quickly agreed to.

In addition to their willingness to allow Prince to fully spread his creative wings, manager at-the-time Owen Husney further recalled that "while everybody was wining, dining, giving us lunches, and promising us homes in Beverly Hills, Russ was the man who took us back to his house, sat on the floor, and talked music with us...There was a real genuine bonding there." Prince's deal with Warner Bros., inked on June 25th, 1977, included an $80,000 advance against 3 studio LPs to be delivered within 26 months, including the first within 6 months of the signing date, each album designated for a $60,000 recording budget. In terms of how the reality of the deal impacted him personally, Prince years later recalled that "once I made it, got my first record contract, got my name on a piece of paper and a little money in my pocket...I was eating every day, I became a much nicer person."

"I used to tease a lot of journalists early on…because I wanted them to concentrate on the music and not so much on me coming from a broken home. I really didn't think that was important. What was important was what came out of my system that particular day. I don't live in the past. I don't play my old records for that reason. I make a statement, then move on to the next."

—Prince

Chapter 8:

For You—1978

With Tommy Vicari settled on as executive producer, Prince entered the Record Plant in Sausalito, CA to commence work on his debut LP, *'For You'*, which Prince would recall years later "I did completely alone." The latter statement applied strictly in a musical context, as manager Owen Husney painted the picture of a group effort that was invested in keeping Prince focused during the recording of his first LP, beginning with Husney and his wife, Prince and E.P. Tommy Vicari all moving into a rental overlooking San Francisco Bay together during the recording sessions. As Husney recalled, "it was a really cool house…It was built close to Sausalito where the Record Plant was. The basic decision was to keep Prince focused on what he was doing. We stayed a little isolated so he could just focus on the album." Of the studio, in-house engineer Steve Fontano recalled that "I think he was impressed with the set-up. It was a very professional studio with 24-track and platinum records on the wall."

Recording began in principle on October 1st, 1977, and though Prince may have had a support staff of sorts guarding after Warner Bros. recording investment, as engineer Steve Fontano recalled, in the studio, Prince very much ran his own show, such that where E.P. Tommy Vicari's input was concerned, "Prince knew what he wanted to hear…The situation didn't allow Tommy to be an opinionated producer. And Prince is not the kind of artist who asks 'Well, what do you think?'…He kind of looked at Tommy and said 'Oh, the babysitter's here, Dad's home.' " Where Fontano did recall Vicari being most useful was on a technical front, such that the engineer recalled "Tommy was making sure everything was recorded properly…and put on tape in a professional manner… The technical aspects were new to him, so he was watching Tommy." Elaborating further, manager Owen Husney added that after a couple of weeks of watching Vicari work the console, Prince "had absorbed everything he needed out of Tommy Vicari's brain… Prince's greatest ability is that he's a sponge, and he can absorb anything from anybody." Concurring, engineer Steve Fontana recalled that Prince "absorbed things and learned very quickly."

In the course of clarifying why creative control in the studio was of such paramount importance to him, Prince explained years later that, leading up to the recording of '*For You*,' "I worked a long time under a lot of different people, and most of the time I was doing it their way. I mean, that was cool, but you know, I figured if I worked hard enough and kept my head straight, one day I'd get to do this on my own…and that's what happened… I think that's the main reason artists fail when they try to play all the instruments is because either than can't play all of the instruments really well—there is usually a flaw somewhere—or they don't play with the same intensity on each track… So I feel like… if I don't try to hurt nobody…and like I say…keep my head on straight… my way usually is the best way." Where Prince might have felt adversarial with Executive Producer Tommy Vicari, engineer Steve Fontano revealed that his own rapport with the brooding genius developed much more smoothly, recalling that while "it took Prince a couple of weeks to sort of warm up to us…After that, we got along really cool. We were basically the same age and after a while we became good friends; he was shy and quiet, but also very confident and very aware of his capabilities."

The tracking process averaged 12 hours at a clip, and typically involved Prince working on one song at a time, beginning with his laying the drum tracks, then synthesizer, bass, and finally rhythm and lead guitar tracks, with engineer Steve Fontano recalled that "he seemed to be one of these guys who could hear the entire song in his head, before he even played it." Playing 25 instruments in sum, including an Oberheim Synthesizer, Guitar (Acoustic), Bass, Guitar, Bass, Drums, Keyboards, Wind, Clavinet, Moog Synthesizer, Synthesizer Bass, Finger Cymbals, Syndrum, Arp Pro Soloist, and Arp String Ensemble among others, Prince would later quip that "I was a physical wreck when I finished that record." Placing a heavy emphasis on the Oberheimer synthesizer during recording, Prince's fanzine Uptown later explained that "Prince uses the synth as the main instrument, playing chords, fills, and lead lines, showing that synths were for more than making weird sound effects or playing solos. His technique of layering synths and incorporating fluid synth lines, often replacing traditional horn lines, became known as the *Minneapolis sound*." In explaining what drove him musically to create the aforementioned signature hometown sound, Prince recalled that in the course of recording *For You*, "I wanted to make a different-sounding record…We originally planned to use horns. But it's really hard to sound different if you use the same instruments…So I created a different kind of horn section by multi-tracking a synthesizer and some guitar lines. I got hip to Polymoogs when I was here working at Sound 80. I was trying to get away from using the conventional sound of piano and Clavinets as the main keyboards."

Once he'd completed principle instrumental tracking, Prince flew out hometown engineer, David 'Z' Rivkin to engineer the album's vocal sessions, with Rivkin recalling that "Prince, because of our work together on his demos, had realized that I was suited to doing the vocals with him…Tommy Vicari was primarily an engineer. He needed help with the vocals. I also think that Prince wanted more input on the experimentation side, and basically that's what I did." When seeking inspiration in the studio during vocal tracking, engineer Steve Fontana recalled that "I think he borrowed a lot from Chaka Khan, in terms of the style of harmonies he would pick...He'd always be listening to her. Chaka Khan was a very big influence. He absolutely loved that girl."

In terms of specific songs Prince labored on vocally, '*For You*' featured an acapella vocal which Prince over-dubbed 46 different times, due to what manager Owen Husney recalled as a work ethic wherein "he wanted everything to be just right...Prince, obviously, is a perfectionist." Putting that thoroughness in a musical context, vocal engineer recalled that while tracking his leads, Prince "wanted to do it so good that he kept doing things over and over." Elaborating in his own words on the toll the extraordinary effort he invested into perfecting his debut LP vocals had on him physically, Prince recalled later that "with a higher voice, it was easier to hit the higher notes...And it also hurts to sing in my lower voice, when I sing too hard. I couldn't get any life, so to speak. The energy, I couldn't get it from that voice."

In addition to the thrill of recording his first major label studio LP in a state of the art studio, Prince also had the opportunity via engineer Steve Fontano to meet one of his adolescent idols, Sly of Sly and the Family Stone, with Fontano recalling that "Prince asked me to introduce him to Sly. So I went to Sly, who is in one of his 'moods,' and didn't feel like meeting anyone. I begged him, 'Man, for me, come on Sly, please! Just go ahead and say 'hi' to the guy. He's a genius, he's fucking great!' Finally, Sly agreed. He walked in, just sort of said 'Hey, what's going on?' Prince was playing the keyboards and got up and shook Sly's hand."

Completed following six months and around $170,000 worth of work, Prince later recalled that *For You* took as long as it did to record because "I was younger then." Returning to Minneapolis from California following the completion of recording in February, 1978, Prince's homecoming, as former bandmate/drummer Charles Smith recalled, was akin to "someone coming home from the Army...We sat in Andre's living room. Me and Andre, and the whole Anderson family. He played the finished album, and it was like angels singing. It brought tears to our eyes. Prince just sort of sat there, kinda sky-like but very proud." In terms of how his family felt, father Roger T. Nelson seemed to feel proudest that his son had successfully followed through with a dream that had originally been his own—to '*make it*' as a professional musician, explaining that "nobody else has ever listened to what I do and did anything about it. I played in a lot of places, they said go home and practice. They couldn't follow—he listened."

Released commercially on April 8ᵗʰ, 1978, '*For You*' debuted at #21 on the Billboard R&B Album Chart, selling a respectable 150,000 copies in the U.S., and 430,000 copies worldwide. Producing the R&B radio hit, '*Soft & Wet*,' which peaked at # 12 on the same genre Singles Chart, the critical reviews of 'For You' spoke as much of things to come for Prince as they did of his first LP, which *Rolling Stone Magazine* noted "introduced his erotic approach" to playing a style of music that *Billboard Magazine/All Music Guide* concluded reflected "staggering talents…(and) shows exceptional skill for arranging and performing mainstream urban R&B and funk." Taking the critical analysis one step further, longtime Janet Jackson producer Jimmy Jam-who came up as a teenager playing with Prince as part of the famed Uptown live music scene—recalled that perhaps the album's most significant impact came locally with its national release, of offering that, thereafter, Prince was revered among his peers because "not only did he make it out of here but he established a sound which I think a lot of people in Minneapolis were going for, which was a very keyboard-dominated sound." Ultimately, the album marked the beginning of a new era of pop music which fused funk, new wave, rock, and pop in a blend that the world hadn't heard before, let alone coming from a one-man band who had everyone universally concluded, had just begun to play…

"Prince arrived on the scene in the late Seventies, and it didn't take long for him to upend the music world with his startling music and arresting demeanor...His first two albums, For You (1978) and Prince (1979), unveiled a budding genius and one-man band."

— Rock & Roll Hall of Fame

Chapter 9:

Prince—1979

Prince would follow up his debut, *'For You,'* just a year later with his sophomore LP, beginning a release routine that would keep Warner Bros. and millions of fans on their toes for years to come. Seeking to build momentum following the crack in the cross-over door 'Soft and Wet' had provided, Prince began work on his self-titled follow-up album at his new home on 5215 France Avenue in Edina, a middle-class Minneapolis suburb, purchased following the release of his first LP. Other changes that had followed with Prince's first taste of success included parting ways with Owen Husney, and inking a new management deal in 1979 with high-profile artist management firm Cavallo and Ruffalo.

Handling Prince's day-to-day artist management was industry vet Steve Fargnoli, who Prince connected to in part via his past-management of Sly and the Family Stone. Farngoli would later explain that his management strategy for Prince was based around taking maximized advantage of the fact that, from day one, "(he was) a pure musician and artist who is so much more prolific than your average rock star...Where other guys go out and buy cars and buy drugs and buy jets...This kid is not interested in that. He's interested in things that satisfy his creative urge." Ambitiously pursuing a bonafied hit single, Prince spent months in-between touring stints tracking in his basement on a TEAC 4-Track reel-to-reel portable home recording studio, penning, producing and performing demos for future hits-to-be including *'I Wanna Be Your Lover,'* *'Why You Wanna Treat Me So Bad?'*, and *'I Feel For You.'* Even by this early point in his still-fledgling career, the latter task came easily to Prince, with the artist explaining that "I knew how to write hits by my second album."

According to former bandmate/cousin Charles Smith, "Prince started shaping the second album when he moved into the house on France Avenue," and upon completing his demos, was soon shuttled off to L.A. by Warner Bros. in April, 1979 to begin proper recording at Alpha Studios with engineer Gary Brandt, who recalled that "I recorded the entire Prince album. Everything we cut was used on his album. He did his demos at his home in Minneapolis." Detailing a routine of 12-hour recording sessions that usually occurred in the evening, Brandt recalled that Prince "was a night person a lot of the time...I thought he was a very sort of secretive guy...(One) of his requests (was)...no chicks allowed in the studio."

Prince's aforementioned hyper-focus, according to Brandt, made the 30-day recording marathon go relatively smoothly because "he already had everything in his head...He knew where the parts were going so it was just basically getting it onto tape. But being an improvisational artist, he always tried to improve on what he heard in his head. His tracks were simple and he didn't really need alot of tracks... We recorded the album 16-track, 2-inch at his request." Utilizing just 16 of Brandt's 24-track studio, Prince recorded his sophomore LP on an *API console,* with Brandt adding from a technical angle that "we actually built our console ground up using some API components but it was our own design and way hot-rodded from a stock API."

Detailing his impressions of Prince's musicianship as the pair worked through tracking over the course of the album's nine tracks, engineer Gary Brandt recalled that "actually drums were his best instrument... He was an extremely good pocket drummer...keyboard player and guitar player... Prince always had a strong hook and very rock oriented rhythms...I remember him making excuses for his guitar playing before he pulled out his Stratocaster and began overdubbing...It is true he would be hard, if not impossible to duplicate."

When attention turned to vocals, Brandt explained that he found Prince's approach to recording "very strange...He'd have me put a microphone right above him while he lay on a blanket beneath my piano. His vocals were very light. He'd tell me where he wanted microphone pick-ups made and I'd advise him from time to time. As long as my suggestions didn't infringe too much on his musical direction, he was reasonably open-minded. I showed him a lot of different little echoes, delays, things that I don't even think he knew about." Finding a balance between where his opinions were and weren't welcomed, Brandt found that even on the technical side where Prince was learning as he went, the artist's sonic instincts usually won out, with the engineer offering the album's breakout hit, '*I Wanna Be Your Lover*' as an instance wherein "we had one conversation about snare mics once after I recorded IWTBYL where he wanted an SM57. On IWTBYL I used a customized AKG 452 and it sounded great...but I did as he asked as the rest of the tracks...(and we) did use his drums."

As principle tracking neared its completion, Prince's work with engineer Gary Brandt ended ahead of its proper conclusion due to what the engineer recalled as a scheduling conflict that grew out of "his managers...(insisting) that I give Prince any amount of time in the studio to mix the album...cancel everything, and give it all to Prince." Recording eventually moved over to Hollywood Sound Recorders, with Brandt conceding in hindsight that "it was too bad. I liked the project and think Prince would have liked to have stayed and finished it." Prince finished the album's principle recording with staff engineer Bob Mockler, who recalled that "the Prince album came to me unfinished...All the basic tracks were cut, but it needed some overdubs and the mix...The tracks were almost complete, but not quite. It lacked some lead vocals and guitar work. There were two or three songs which didn't need any overdubs."

Working roughly 2 more weeks on overdubbing, followed by a marathon 9-day mix session for the album's 9 songs, Mockler recalled that "once we got into mixing, we mixed them very quickly. We were definitely nailing them. He had spent so much time on his first album that he just wanted the new album out...Our competition on that album was Michael Jackson and Kool and the Gang, and I think we looked them right in the eye." Still, once the album had entered the mixing phase of the recording process, Mockler took the opportunity to refine some of the album's lengthier sonic affairs, including 'Sexy Dancer,' which Mockler recalled went under the chopping block because "Prince didn't know what to leave in and what to take out...I thought the keyboard solo was the one to go for. Prince didn't understand editing, but I knew where to cut so it was least intrusive. The only reason he knew where the cut was, because he knew the music, but he was still amazed."

Another instance of the latter was '*When We're Dancing Close and Slow,*' which Mockler recalled was a special case wherein "I had to fade every bass note manually. I made the drums extra big on that one because I wanted it to have that pulse. Everything about the song is intimate and I just thought that contrasting that with this big drum sound, at least for those days, was a neat idea." Elaborating on some of the other further developments the album's songs went through in the course of his mixing sessions with Prince, Mockler further recalled that "on '*Still Waiting*,' there was a buzz on the drums. I couldn't get rid of it, so I just left it in. Prince thought the pause when the end of the '*Bambi*' fade hits the beginning of '*Still Waiting*' was perfect...I recorded the guitar solo on '*Bambi*' and I was a big fan of the song. The track blew me away, but he didn't like the way it was going down. Something about the song was rubbing him the wrong way. Maybe because it was too different from the rest of the album. I said 'Prince, let me have a chance to put this one together.' He gave me an afternoon and came back four hours later, listened and said 'Let's do it!' Looking back, it's my favorite song."

As with his debut LP, though best friend and bandmate Andre Cymone was around during recording, Prince still played the album's instruments by himself, later explaining that the only outside musical contribution came "on the second LP...(when) I used André, my bass player, on '*Why You Wanna Treat Me So Bad?*' He sang a small harmony part that you really couldn't hear." Cymone further recalled that "he pretty much did...play everything. You know there was a little bit here and there, but for the most part he played everything and I wouldn't want to take any credit from what he did 'cause I think he did a great job and I was right there. So it's pretty true to what it says, you know, performed, played, produced and all that kind of stuff by Prince."

Prince would later conclude the album was "a piece of cake (to record because I)...knew more about engineering", but his other motivation for taking as little time as he did comparatively to his debut LP came with the realization that "I had to make some money to prove to Warner Bros. that I was a businessman. I spent too much money in the studio for the first album, so they looked at me like, here's a child in here trying to do a man's job. I'm really stubborn and I strive for the best, so I tried to do the best the second time around and make a hit and do it for the least amount of money. My second album cost $35,000, but the first one cost four times that."

Released on October 19th 1979 Prince's self-titled follow-up to '*For You*' debuting at a triumphant #3 on the Billboard Top 20 R&B Album Chart, and quickly going gold, based off the momentum created by the massive radio hit '*I Wanna Be Your Lover*', which *Rolling Stone Magazine* later called "the song that made him a star." Peaking at # 1 on the Billboard R&B Singles Chart, and cracked the top 20 on Billboard's Top 100 Pop Singles Chart, reaching #11, while the album's follow-up single, '*Why You Wanna Treat Me So Bad*', reached # 13 on Billboard's R&B Singles Chart. Critical praise once again abounded, beginning with *Rolling Stone Magazine*'s praise of the fact that "not only does Prince possess the most thrilling R&B falsetto since Smokey Robinson, but this nineteen-year-old Minneapolis-bred *Wunderkind* is his own writer-producer and one-man band, playing synthesizer, guitar, drums and percussion. Whereas Prince's debut album (last year's *For You*) stressed his instrumental virtuosity, Prince teems with hooks that echo everyone from the Temptations to Jimi Hendrix to Todd Rundgren. But Smokey Robinson's classic Motown hits, in which the singer's falsetto signified his erotic thrall, are Prince's chief models... *'I Wanna Be Your Lover'* (Number 11 pop, Number One R&B) and *'Why You Wanna Treat Me So Bad?'* (Number 13 R&B) from Prince (Number 22, 1979) suggested his musical range."

Billboard Magazine/All Music Guide, meanwhile, celebrated Prince's success in "expanding the urban R&B and funk approach of his debut," delivering what the magazine deemed "a considerably more accomplished record than his first effort, featuring the first signs of his adventurous, sexy signature sound... a handful of songs rank as classics. *'I Wanna Be Your Lover'* is excellent lite funk and *'Why You Wanna Treat Me So Bad?'* is a wonderful soulful plea, but *'I Feel for You,'* a sexy slice of urban R&B with a strong pop melody, is the true masterpiece of *Prince*." *Creem Magazine*, meanwhile, predicted that Prince was "going to be a big star, and he deserves it," while the *Los Angeles Times* complimented the fact that "Prince's music can't be pigeonholed into one category, and that's to his benefit." Ultimately, however, *Rolling Stone Magazine* was most dead-on in concluding that "the simplicity of Prince's words, hooks and rhythms are pure pop." Though he had become a bonafied R&B star, pop was the ultimate plateau Prince had his sights set upon, explaining years later that, at the time, he'd "just scratched the surface...There's so many sounds, it's limitless." So too were the boundaries for Prince heading into the 1980s, a decade whose pop landscape would be both shaped and progressed by Prince's quest for what he would later describe as "a higher plain" musically. Without a doubt, *Dirty Mind* would be Prince's first major step toward that next level...

A Look Back
At Prince

Chapter 10:

Dirty Mind–1980

With just his third studio LP, 1980's *Dirty Mind*, Prince was clearly seeking to push pop's boundaries, such that the LP inspired *Rolling Stone Magazine* to point out that "*Dirty Mind* is a pop record of Rabelaisian achievement: entirely, ditheringly obsessed with the body, yet full of sentiments that please and provoke the mind… Nothing…could have prepared us for the liberating lewdness of *Dirty Mind*. Here, Prince lets it all hang out…At its best, *Dirty Mind* is positively filthy…(and) jolts with the unsettling tension that arises from rubbing complex erotic wordplay against clean, simple melodies. Across this electric surface glides Prince's graceful quaver, tossing off lyrics with an exhilarating breathlessness. He takes the sweet romanticism of Smokey Robinson and combines it with the powerful vulgate poetry of Richard Pryor. The result is cool music dealing with hot emotions."

To accomplish what was at the time a singular pop vision, Prince hid away in his home studio, with the aforementioned publication reporting that "he made the album with his own hands, well away from the prying label execs who oversaw the first two." Recalling that at the time, "nobody knew what was going on, and I became totally engulfed in it… It really felt like me for once." In elaborating on his by-then already legendary recording regimen, Prince also addressed why he preferred at the time to record alone, explaining that "the reason I don't use musicians a lot of the time had to do with the hours that I worked. I swear to God it's not out of boldness when I say this, but there's not a person around who can stay awake as long as I can. Music is what keeps me awake…I record when I feel like, and when I have a song in my head. I don't like to have a session at ten in the morning, and conclude at five in the evening. I go into the studio at very strange hours sometimes and do marathon sessions until I'm ready to drop."

Still, Prince further explained that, in spite of his musical high, on a personal down note, "during the *Dirty Mind* period, I would go into fits of depression and get physically ill. I would have to call people to help get me out of it. I don't do that anymore…A lot had to do with the band's situation, the fact that I couldn't make people in the band understand how great we could all be together if we all played our part. A lot had to do with being in love with someone and not getting any love back. And there was the fact that I didn't talk much with my father and sister." That aforementioned emotional disconnect in his personal life informed his professional pursuits in that "when I did other records, I think I was in love, and I wasn't when I did (*Dirty Mind*)." Underscoring the latter point, keyboardist Matt Fink recalled that, prior to the album's recording having begun, Prince was already focused on its writing, recalling that "we were in Orlando, Florida on the Rick James tour, and me and Bobby and Dez were heading out to Disney World, and I asked 'Wanna join us?' So Prince was sitting up outside on a balcony playing his guitar, and he said 'Naw, I'm gonna stay here, working on a new song,' which turned out to be '*When You Were Mine.*' "

In how the latter impacted the album's lyrical content, Prince explained that "it was a revelation recording *Dirty Mind*…I realized that I could write just what was on my mind and things that I'd encountered and I didn't have to hide anything. The lyrics on the new album are straight from the heart, whereas the other albums were more feelings, more dreams and fantasies, and they stuck to the more basic formula that I'd learned through playing Top 40 material in old bands. When you talk about fucking and blow jobs, you cannot constantly hedge on it. You wind up talking crap. That's the kind of hypocrisy I want to expose. I say out loud what no man or woman dares to say, but is thinking about... My songs are more about love than they are about sex...I don't consider myself a great poet, or interpreter a la Moses. I just know I'm here to say what's on my mind, and I'm in a position where I can do that."

In the course of recording what *Rolling Stone Magazine* would later hail as the album's "crisp, artfully constructed compositions," Prince keyboardist Matt 'Dr.' Fink recalled that Prince drew some of the album's musical influences from the "stacks and stacks of records in his house that he got free from Warner Bros...He was listening to just about everything." Fink, who collaborated with Prince on the album's hit title track over the course of the album's recording between the summer of 1979 and 1980, further recalled of the house and its fully-equipped home studio that "was in a house he was renting on the North Arm of Lake Minnetonka, on the Northwestern side, and the studio was comprised of a 16-Track Ampex 2-inch analog deck, just plunked down in the basement, but not really built into the house. The mixing console for tracking purposes was a 16-channel AMEC board, a very heavy-duty board, very high quality and big for a 16-channel board. As far as outboard gear, he had some compressors like an 1176, a couple LA2A teletronics, an Eventide harmonizer, a couple of basic outboard reverbs—like the Lexicons PCM-60s. As far as vocal mics, in those days he was using a U-47 or a Telephunkin, but primarily the Neumann U-47, coupled with GML mic-pre's. He had the drums pre-miced in a separate booth, and the drums were already miced up." Maintenance tech Don Batts further recalled of Prince's home studio that "the kitchen was right there and then you went into his living room and that's where the studio started. The console was rammed up against a table. The Ampex MM1100 tape machine was held together with baling wire and patches...I 'automated'

Prince's home studio so it would function without me. It was all preset so it didn't have to be changed for a session."

Of the duo's collaboration on '*Dirty Mind*,' Fink recalled its evolving out of "a usual warm-up jam session at the beginning of rehearsal in the middle of summer 1979, at the old U Warehouse on Lake Street in South Minneapolis. We were in this big concrete wall room on the 7th floor, really echoy with no soundproofing, so it was really loud and bombastic in there. So we were jamming away, and I was messing around with this chord progression on the ARP Omni String Synthesizer, which was a combination string machine and also had a basic, polyphonic synthesizer section that you could mix in with the strings, so you could get fake analog horn sounds going along with the strings, or synthey pad-like sounds. So I was playing on the Omni, playing this part, and Prince really seemed to like this groove I was working on, and after the rehearsal when everybody had left, he approached me and said he really liked it and asked me to play it again. So then he said 'Let's go out to my house and do something with this track.' So we went out there, and recorded the basic rhythm sections—just the two of us—and he was on drums, I was on keyboards, and there was no bass guitar on the song; it was just a pulsing synth-bass on the ARP Omni, all with the basic chord progression added on top, all at the same time on the machine. While we were recording, basically I just had to hit record when he was laying down the drums, and then he actually laid the drums down first, and had the arrangement going in his head, as to where all the fills go and all that. So I just hit record and got a few takes—maybe two or three—until he got what he wanted. Then I got on the keyboards, and he directed me as to how he wanted the arrangement to go. He also came in and wrote the bridge during that session, he'd asked me to come up with something, and I was drawing a bit of a blank, and so he put something together very quickly. So midnight rolled around, and he dismissed me about then, and the next morning when we got to rehearsal—and we usually started around noon—he showed up with a rough mix of the finished song, and his guitar and vocals had been added. I was very impressed with his quickness."

Elaborating on the latter theme as it played out beyond the studio in all aspects of Prince's life, former manager Steve Fargnoli recalled a work-ethic wherein he was "demanding of himself and of everyone who works around him...You always have to be on your toes. He doesn't play by the rules." Maintenance engineer Don Batts, offering an example of the type of results Prince expected of his studio employees especially, explained in recollection that he'd first been hired after "I walked into a rehearsal, and about 3 minutes later, someone broke a keyboard. So I walked over and unscrewed and fixed that. And it just kind of went on and on through the course of the day. 2 or 3 hours later I was hired." In terms of how Prince's frantic pace impacted his work in the studio, Batts further recalled a sonic serendipity wherein "*Dirty Mind* was real rough but there was just this magic to the whole thing: the one-take magic. I couldn't imagine him going back and re-recording the songs. If it were three takes, it wasn't right and that was very, very rare." *Rolling Stone Magazine*, in musically describing the album's ground-breaking eight tracks, observed that "throughout, Prince's melodies peel back layers of disco rhythm to insert slender, smooth funk grooves and wiggly, hard-rock guitar riffing. In his favorite musical trick, the artist contrasts a pumping, low-toned drum sound with a light, abrupt guitar or keyboard riff pitched as high as his voice (which is often double-tracked to emphasize its airiness). Though Prince is playing everything himself, the result isn't bloodless studio virtuosity. His music attains the warmth and inspiration of a group collaboration because it sounds as if he's constantly competing against himself: Prince the drummer tries to drown out Prince the balladeer, and so forth...powerful as the final moments of *Dirty Mind*, when, during the anti-draft '*Partyup*,' he challenged, 'All lies, no truth/Is it fair to kill the youth?' before defiantly commanding, '*Party up!*' "

Released on October 8th, 1980, Prince made his commercial bones with '*Dirty Mind*,' inspiring *Billboard Magazine* to hail the album as "his first masterpiece, a one-man tour de force of sex and music; it was hard funk, catchy Beatlesque melodies, sweet soul ballads, and rocking guitar pop, all at once." *Rolling Stone*, for its part, highlighted the fact that "*Dirty Mind* signaled some splendidly liberated music to come, not just from Prince but from his few peers, like Michael Jackson...*Dirty*

Mind departed not just from Prince's first LP, of fairly conventional R&B, and his second, Hendrix-infused album, but from most of what else was out there." Of the boundaries that the album's themes pushed lyrically, Prince explained that "when I first played the *Dirty Mind* album for (my father)…he said, 'You're swearing on the record. Why do you have to do that?' And I said, 'Because I swear…When I brought it to the record company it shocked a lot of people…But they didn't ask me to go back and change anything, and I'm real grateful. Anyway, I wasn't being deliberately provocative. I was being deliberately *me*." In defending the album's musical integrity, the latter-mentioned publication pointed out that, ultimately, the album worked because it was "lewdness cleansed by art, with joy its socially redeeming feature. *Dirty Mind* may be dirty, but it certainly isn't pornographic."

Prince's willingness to push pop's boundaries outward would inspire the Rock & Roll Hall of Fame years later to report that, at the turn of the decade, "interest in the youthful rising star was further kindled by *Dirty Mind*, a provocative and sinuously funky album that appeared like a directional marker at the start of the Eighties." *Entertainment Weekly*, meanwhile, complimented the record as "the punchiest production and writing of his early career ('*When You Were Mine*,' '*Dirty Mind*'), complete with over-the-top lyrics ('*Sister*,' '*Head*')-a masterwork of lewdness and desire." For his own part, Prince, when asked at the time what he thought distinguished his sound from anything else out on the radio in 1980, reasoned that "I guess it's just the basic sound. It's hard to classify Earth, Wind and Fire, for instance, but you can always tell it's them. It's not a brand of music, it's a group sound, an identity of their own. Maybe it's my voice, or just my total sound, who knows?…(With *Dirty Mind*), I wanted to go develop a following that would see me as me and not just the guy with a Top 10 record." Prince's following consisted not just of the million-plus fans at the time who bought the album, but also an ever-growing chorus of critical admirers, including *Billboard Magazine*, who ultimately concluded that *Dirty Mind* was "a breathtaking, visionary album, and its fusion of synthesizers, rock rhythms, and funk set the style for much of the urban soul and funk of the early '80s."

"Prince, by taking on social issues…assumes his place in the pantheon of Sly Stone inspired Utopian funksters like Rick James and George Clinton"

—Rolling Stone Magazine

Chapter 11:

Controversy—1981

Seeking to expand on the barriers he'd begun to knock down with *'Dirty Mind'* with his fourth studio LP, aptly titled *'Controversy,'* Prince, according to *Rolling Stone Magazine* in their 5-star review of the album, by "taking on social issues…assumes his place in the pantheon of Sly Stone inspired Utopian funksters like Rick James and George Clinton… Prince stands as Stone's most formidable heir." Still, in spite of critical comparisons to pop provocateurs past, Prince explained that "all the way back in *Controversy*, I was trying to break from the hallucination. People said, 'This is what's hittin' now, Prince.' But I wasn't paying attention to that. Duke Ellington never changed. Miles Davis never changed. Their work is intact."

While he had included Dr. Fink as a collaborator on the title track to *Dirty Mind*, on the majority of *Controversy*, Prince once again recorded the majority of the album's music alone in the studio, conceding years later that "I was horrible. To be perfectly honest, I was surrounded by my friends, but nevertheless, we had a difference of opinion in a lot of situations—musically speaking, that is. A lot had to do with me not being quite sure exactly which direction I wanted to go in." Still, the progress he'd made in loosening up that rule with Dirty Mind prepared Prince to keep moving in a more collaborative direction, such that "later on, toward the *Controversy* period, I got a better grip on that. That's when we started to see more and more people participating in recording activities." For those portions of *Controversy* that Prince tracked by himself at his home studio, now located in his newly purchased 2-story ranch house on Lake Riley in Chanhassen (eventually painted Purple), sometime engineer David Rivkin recalled of the new home studio that "it was a big control room, pretty much full blown. He had huge speakers and it was designed to be a control room. The recording area was fairly small. The recording rooms were small, more like small booths." While most of his instruments were housed in the basement studio, Prince also had set up a Yamaha grand piano in the upstairs living room, hooked into the studio so he could record himself.

Following the completion of initial home studio recording sessions in the spring and early summer of 1981, Prince headed out to L.A. in August of 1981 to commence principle work on the album's recording. Initially working at Hollywood Sound for roughly a week with engineer Bob Mockler, who recalled being wildly impressed upon a first listen to some of the demos—including the album's title track—*Controversy*, such that "I asked him 'Where did you do this?' He said, 'I did it at home.' He had done the track completely by himself in his home studio." Getting immediately down to work, Mockler conveyed a feeling of awe at watching Prince at work, such that "(I felt) I was sitting in the studio with a modern-day Mozart...He came in and plays the drums and you wouldn't be hearing anything but the drums. The tape would be virgin! Then he'd put everything to the drums: bass, keyboards, guitar and background vocals. Once he got the backing tracks down, he did a serious lead vocal. He's the only musician I've ever worked with that I never saw guessing once...We just worked so fast together...It was just him and me in there. Prince would just go and put the drum part on the tape, and then he'd put everything to the drums, playing a bass part, then a keyboard part, then a guitar part background vocals, and a rough lead vocal. Everything was in his head. We're out of there in a day with a finished track!"

Following completion of work on album keepers including *'Let's Work,'* *'Ronnie, Talk to Russia,'* and *'Do Me Baby,'* Prince and Mockler parted company following the artist's decision to head back to Minneapolis, before deciding to move operations from Hollywood Sound Recorders to Sunset Sound Studios. His engineering co-pilot upon moving studios, in-house Sunset Sound engineer Ross Pallone, recalled that "when he came into town to do that record, the studio manager sent me out to LAX to pick him up, and I remember trying to generate a conversation with him in the car, and he didn't really want to talk much. So I had the radio on, and said 'Prince, what other kind of music do you like that's on the radio?', and he said 'Well, I hardly ever listen to the radio, I don't pay much attention to other people's music.' " Picking up quickly on the fact that Prince's hyper-focus on recording permeated every aspect of his life, Pallone also explained on a personal level that "Prince doesn't talk much, he is very quiet and hardly gives up anything. He never initiates conversations. He was just real to himself, real quiet, didn't share feelings or anything about his life, and didn't really communicate much—other than telling me 'This is what I want to do, let's do it,' just very business-like."

In spite of their lack of non-musical personal interaction, Pallone explained that "the whole time Prince was in the Sunset Sound working on the album, I was the engineer on the sessions; there was no assistant, it was just him and I." Recognizing that Prince's genius was always busy at work, the engineer also recalled at the time feeling as though "he was a very different person, I'd never met anyone like him before. Very non-conversational, didn't really say too much other than what he wanted, and he would be pretty specific, and then I would provide it for him. But we didn't sit down ahead of entering the studio to have a conversation about the concept of the record, or what he was planning on doing." To allow himself full freedom to spread his creative wings, Pallone explained that Prince "had a lockout session at Sunset Sound, wherein he had that studio 24 hours a day for as long as they wanted. Prince likes to go into the studio and do whatever he wants, and he could have anything equipment-wise he wanted set up in there—be it outboard gear or musical instruments—and no one could touch it. Because at that time in the music business, much different than it is now, if there wasn't a lockout, we were doing 2 sessions a day—a 10-6 session, and 7-whenever—the studio was very busy. So when Prince was there, it was very much just his studio."

Detailing Prince's technical set-up at Sunset Sound, engineer Ross Pallone recalled that "Prince had Studio B, which was our larger room. That room could be whatever you wanted, it was a pretty good-sized room, and we had half of it carpeted, and then the back-half of the room was a slate-floor, with wood on some of the walls, and the back wall was an all rock finish. So we recorded him in the live area of the room. The studio had a custom console that was originally made by Buschnell, and that console had API equalizers in it, Gensen Transformers, and Penny & Giles faders. We used a 16 track 3M Multi-Track machine to do the basics, and then we added another 24 track slave machine, that we locked up to the 16 track, and what we'd do is he'd record till he ran out of tracks on the 16 track, then we'd bounce those over to the 24 track locked up, and he would continue to work on the 24 track. Then when it came down to mixdown time, we'd lock those 2 machines back together and he would use those 2 machines to mix from. The mixdown tape machine would have been another 3M 2-half inch 2-Track machine."

Prince's recording routine, as Pallone recalled it, began "basically with him telling me we were going to have a 4 o'clock start each day. So I would be in there at 4, then he would show up sometime between 8 and 10, and we would work all night. I worked on the record with him for a couple months, most of a summer. I remember going home to my house between 4 and 6 in the morning, and sleeping till about 2, then going back to the studio every day. He was definitely a night-guy in the studio." Atmospherically, the engineer recalled that "Prince kept the room pretty dark, some candles, some incense, that kind of a vibe. He was a very nice guy and very even tempered, and we didn't really have much in the way of breakdowns or problems. I was able to give him what he wanted and he was very nice, just was a quiet guy. It's hard to describe somebody like that, he just really didn't communicate once. I never had a problem where he was upset at me or mad at me. He was easy to work with, you just had to accept the way he was and how he wanted to work, and I was very impressed. He was a phenomenal musician, no matter what instrument he picked up—whether it was keyboards or bass or drums or guitar—he looked like a guy who'd been playing those instruments for 30 years. He was very relaxed in the studio and could do anything. He just wanted to do everything himself, and was capable." Prior to Prince picking up any instrument, he and Pallone would first work on micing, with the engineer recalling that "he was always pretty happy with the sounds I got for him, he didn't really make me make a lot of changes. On every instrument he played—bass, drums, guitar, keyboards—I would get the sounds for him. And getting sounds for him went pretty quickly."

As always, Prince began his recording process by tracking drums, with Pallone describing a micing set-up wherein "we used AKG 414s for the overheads, Shure 57s on the snare, top and bottom, that was typical of the day, a Sennheiser 451 on the kick-drum, on the toms we had 414s, and at the time, room mics weren't the big thing, so we didn't use room mics to my recollection." Next, as Pallone recalled, "Prince would say 'Ross, I'd like to record drums,' so we'd get the drums set up, I'd mic the drums, and I would get him his drum sound—although he tuned his own drums—and he would go out and play, come back in and listen to the sound, and tell me if he was happy or not with it. Then he would lay down the drum track, and basically would work on one song at a time. So he'd go out and record the drums for the whole song, and he didn't use a click track. He played alone, and I remember being so impressed with his being an extremely great musician. I've worked with some great musicians at that time, and he was amazing, very very good at everything he played. His meter was dead on. He was pretty quick at tracking drums, maybe two or three takes and that was it. He knew in his mind exactly what he wanted."

In the tradition of his past album recording sessions, Pallone recalled that "once he'd laid down a drum track, he'd usually lay down the guitar next, and then go to bass. It was interesting too because after he did the drum tracks for each song, he'd track everything else in the control room. So we'd set up the guitar amps out in the studio, then run cables into the control room, and then I'd set him up with a remote control for the multi-track machine, and he would stand there with his guitar, and I'd get the sound for him. Once he was happy with the sound, he'd excuse me from the studio, and say 'Go ahead and go to the lounge, and I'll call you when I need you.' Then he'd sit there and play guitar til he was happy with the take. Then he'd call me back in the studio, so he would do ALL his own punching in, and at the time we didn't have auto-punch like you do now with Protools. So I was amazed at watching him play guitar then reach over the locator and punch himself in, and continue to play. He was very good at it. Then when he was done with guitar track, he'd call me in and say 'I want to do another guitar track.' That stuff took him a little longer, sometimes he would work on a guitar track for several hours." Continuing, Pallone explained that Prince typically would next say 'I want to do bass now', then I'd set up the bass sound, and it would be the same routine. For bass, we used to record direct, and he played a Fender bass and Fender Stratocaster guitar. He'd say, 'I'll call you when I need you,' and work on tracking the song's bass part."

When Prince turned his attention to tracking the album's considerable keyboard presence, which *Billboard Magazine* termed a "fascination with synthesizers and synthesizing disparate pop music genres," Pallone recalled that "after tracking guitars, he would play keyboards, we had everything all set up in the control room, so he had the same routine: he'd punch in everything himself for the keyboard parts, unless he had a problem where he couldn't punch it in himself, then I would come in help, but it was rare. I believe the synthesizer was an Oberheim OB 8. I don't think he thought that deeply about sounds before he came in, the keyboard had a lot of pre-programmed sounds, stock sounds that come in the keyboard, and then he would tweak on them til he found whatever sound he wanted to lay down on a track." Prince, for his own part, explained that in choosing which synthesizers he chose to utilize in conjunction with the album's mix of live and programmed drums, "I'll listen to the kick drum. The bass guitar won't go as deep as the synth, and the kick drum tells me how deep I have to go. My original drum machine, the Linn, had only one type of kick. I think I had *the* first Linn. I did '*Private Joy*' with a prototype of that Linn." Of the latter sound, which would become a blueprint of sorts for Prince's future drum sound, drummer Bobby Z recalled sensing that Prince was onto something, such that "when I heard '*Private Joy*' for the first time, that's when I knew things were going to change…He told me right away I was gonna play pads hooked up to the drum machine. It was the very first time I heard the Linn drum machine. It was his first attempt at using it and I thought it came out pretty well."

Of the album's vocals, which inspired *Rolling Stone Magazine* to comment in their review of the LP that "Prince is…an extraordinary singer whose falsetto, at its most tender, recalls Smokey Robinson's sweetness; At its most brittle, Prince's voice sounds like Sylvester at his ironic and challenging best," engineer Ross Pallone recalled that the artist's vocal recording routine was "a pretty interesting process actually, because he wanted to do it in the control room and he wanted to do it alone. I was never in the room with him when he was recording vocals, except for getting the sound, so once he would start tracking his vocals in earnest, I would leave the control room. What I did was set him up with an AKG C-12 Tube microphone, right at the console, with the mic hanging right in front of him on a stand, and then we had Oratone speakers—which were the small speakers at the time—and he would play whatever track he was working on through the Oratones and sing. No headphones, with the speakers on while he sang. There was some leakage, but he accepted it, he was okay with it. Suprisingly not that much leakage, the microphone was carteoid, and the speakers weren't big speakers, there were little 3-inch tones on those speakers, so there wasn't a lot of bass response out of them. And I don't believe he was playing the speakers that loud, just loud enough for him to hear the track. And that's how he did all the vocals. All of the effects he applied came during mixing, so he recorded vocals with no effects."

Transitioning into what engineer Ross Pallone regarded as perhaps the most sonically involved part of the pair's record-making process—mixing—the engineer began by explaining that, much to his chagrin, "when the mix process started, Prince became a little bit more communicative with me." When discussing how Prince attained what *Billboard Magazine* described as the album's ground-breaking "new wave-tinged funk" sound, Pallone explained that "one of the biggest factors in how he got the sound that he got on that record was tape compression, so in other words, there's meters on the tape machine and he totally ignored the meters. When we mixed, everything went into the red all the time, from start to finish of the song, and that created what engineers called tape compression. So the tape would get saturated with signal, to the point where it can't have dynamics. So now adays, people with digital have programs they can use to simulate that sound, but the tape has a certain sound that it gets when you overload it with signal. And Prince was not only overloading the tape, he would also overload the mix console, which was on purpose. So some of the qualities you're hearing on his voice have mainly to do with tape compression, the overloading of the console, and the fact that he had recorded all his vocal tracks with the Oratone speakers on in the same room he was recording them in, that would contribute to the sound of the vocal."

Elaborating on their mixing process for the album's vocal tracks, Pallone described a set-up for a very hands-on Prince wherein "what I would do is set up the console with different effects, and show him how to work each of the effects, and then just like the recording of the vocals. Once I had him set up, I would pull a mix up for him, get it started and maybe spend an hour or two on a mix for him, getting it to sound where I thought it sounded good, then I would leave and he would finish it up. Then when he was ready to go to tape with it, he would call me in and I would record it to the 2-track, then we would go through the listen-back process, and then once he was happy, he might do a few more mixes of the same song, keep them all overnight, and then choose which he wanted to go with as the finished track." In terms of which of Sunset Sound's specific effects Prince utilized in the course of mixing his vocals, Pallone recalled that "I don't think he used any reverb on his voice at all, and we had two live chambers there ready to go. Back then, there weren't as many effects as there are available today, so we had the 2 live chambers, 3 EMTs or plates that we could use for reverb, and then we'd add Early

Even Tide equipment, which would have been a 910 Harmonizer, and we also had an instant planter, and a Delta T digital delay."

Atmospherically, as it had been with recording, Pallone recalled that "back then, during the mix-down process, Prince kept it very dark in the studio, some candles, and he would work on a mix for quite a while, many hours to get the mix the way he wanted it. Prince mixed a lot different from my taste in how I would have approached it. He mixed on the Oratone speakers just BLASTING loud. I would walk into the room and the round speakers were like oval because they were pulsating and so distorted. He liked that generally, and every now and then, he'd listen to a song on the big speakers, but not that much. He mostly listened on the little Oratones. The entire mixing process probably took 2 or 3 weeks, which was typical, especially with analog mixing. At that time, we didn't have automation on that console, so everything had to be done by hand. He would play with the EQs, and get the mix he wanted. He rarely had anyone come into the studio, he was pretty much a loner—he didn't have guests, or an entourage, or girls hanging out. It was very much business, work. When Prince was done, he was just done. So there wasn't any kind of conversation or celebration, or anything like that of the record's being done."

Looking back on the once-in-a-lifetime experience—if nothing more than in terms of the unique process—of recording with Prince, engineer Ross Pallone, whose extensive client list over the years has also included collaborations with such stars as Michael McDonald and Earth Wind and Fire, concluded that Prince was, by far, "the most different person I've ever worked with—except for Michael Jackson. Definitely one of the more advanced musicians I have worked with. I'd put him in the category of Michael Jackson, who I worked with quite a bit, with his vocals and his ears, and knowing what he wanted in his head. With Michael Jackson, being that he didn't play instruments, he would have to communicate that to other people, Prince didn't. Michael would say exactly what he wanted, sing the guitar riffs to the guitar player, until the guy would play what he sang. That's the way Michael worked, of course Prince did it himself. But even with talents being different, I would put them both on the same par like that."

Released on October 14ᵗʰ, 1981, *Rolling Stone Magazine* would later report that "*Controversy* (Number 21, 1981) had two hits, the title cut (# 3, R&B, 1981) and '*Let's Work*' (# 9, 1982)," further pushing Prince toward the forefront of a new wave/pop genre he was already playing a heavy hand in shaping, further inspiring the aforementioned publication in its review of the LP to compliment Prince as a "consummate master of pop-funk song forms and a virtuosic multi-instrumentalist." Heading into 1982, Prince would begin crafting his mainstream commercial break-through LP with *1999*, which *Rolling Stone*'s Album Guide would later conclude "may be Prince's most influential album: Its synth-and-drum machine-heavy arrangements codified the 'Minneapolis sound' that loomed over mid-'80s R&B and pop, not to mention the next two decades' worth of electro, house, and techno."

> "*Perhaps more than any other artist, Prince called the tune for pop music in the Eighties, imprinting his Minneapolis sound on an entire generation of musicians both black and white.*"
>
> —Rolling Stone Magazine

"He was trying to become as mainstream as possible without compromising."
—Revolution keyboardist Matt 'Dr.' Fink

Chapter 12:

1999—1982

Building off the momentum he'd begun with '*Dirty Mind*,' according to *Rolling Stone Magazine*, by the arrival of 1999 in 1982, "Prince, at the tender age of twenty-two…(had) become the inspiration for a growing renegade school of Sex & Funk & Rock & Roll…(With) this two-LP set of artfully arranged synthesizer pop…having graduated in record time from postdisco garage rock to high-tech studio wizardry, Prince works like a colorblind technician who's studied both Devo and Afrika Bambaataa and the Soul Sonic Force, keeping the songs constantly kinetic with an inventive series of shocks and surprises." This praise fit precisely with Prince's goal with each album of "always (trying)…to do something different and conquer new ground."

Perhaps the greatest surprise to the growing legions of fans and especially critics paying closer and closer attention to Prince's ascension toward superstardom was the introduction of a band, later to be named the Revolution, who even managed to show up in light musical touches throughout the album, including keyboardist Lisa Coleman and guitarist Dez Dickerson each getting a lead line in the album's title track and lead-off single, with tour manager Alan Leeds recalling the origins of the shared-vocal decision as one Prince made by first having himself, Dez Dickerson and Lisa Coleman sing "the entire song together…By the time he mixed it, Prince had changed his mind and decided to split up the lines, passing the baton among the singers like a relay race. The unusual approach accounts for how the melody keeps changing—as some of what are now lead vocals had been performed as harmonies." Still, the rare and relatively new presence of outside musicians on his studio recordings signaled that Prince, as he explained it, "wanted community more than anything else…We've all used shock value to sell things…I used shock to get attention. But back when I was doing the freaky songs in the freaky outfits, we were exploring ideas. I wanted my band to be multiracial, male and female, to reflect society."

Debuting a new band in the course of *1999* that was composed of—Dez Dickerson on guitar, Brown Mark on bass, Bobby Z. on drums & percussion, Lisa Coleman on keyboards and piano, and Matt 'Dr.' Fink on keyboards—essentially the same line-up that on the next album be introduced as the Revolution, minus guitarist Dez Dickerson's replacement by Wendy Melvoin. In detailing what he felt each band member brought to the table in both suiting his singular style of playing, and beyond in their performance as a band, Prince began at the time by explaining that "I personally love this band more than any other group I've ever played with for that reason. Everybody knows what they have to do. I know there's something I have to do…Bobby Z was the first one to join. He's my best friend. Though he's not such a spectacular drummer, he watches me like no other drummer would. Sometimes, a real great drummer, like Morris Day, will be more concerned with the lick he is doing as opposed to how I am going to break it down… Mark Brown's just the best bass player I know, period. I wouldn't have anybody else. If he didn't play with me, I'd eliminate bass from my music. Same goes for Matt. He's more or less a technician. He can read and write like a whiz, and is one of the fastest in the world." Of Lisa Coleman, Prince revealed that "Lisa is like my sister. She'll play what the average person won't. She'll press two notes with one finger so the chord is a lot larger, things like that. She's more abstract. She's into Joni Mitchell, too…(She) had this way of playing chords that were so perfect… Lisa was never an explosive keyboard player, but she was a master of color in her harmonies; I could sing off of what she had with straight soul." Elaborating further on what he felt Lisa brought to the group, drummer Bobby Z observed that "Lisa is a great musician, really talented. She was a different kind of musician, more chordal and moody. She added color to the music. I thought she was a better compliment to Matt, and I thought she was mysterious and interesting. Prince loved her voice even though she was primarily hired for her keyboard playing…Lisa sang with a monotone-sounding voice which worked much better with Prince's new sound."

In offering further commentary on how the group worked within Prince's unique one-man band formula, keyboard player Matt 'Dr.' Fink recalled that, on a routine basis, "Prince would always move around the instruments during rehearsal and play different things—bass, guitars, drums keyboards—and was always showing people parts or just doing it to keep his own chops up. He would always get on the drums at some point, and we used to jam some pretty serious fusiony-jazz stuff with him where technically he was playing some things that were on a level with some of the better fusion-jazz drummers of the day." Offering another band member's perspective, drummer Bobby Z conceded that it presented "a very rare and unusual situation…You're dealing with a situation where the guy can play all the instruments. He can do it fast. He hears it in his head. If he can teach you a part and you have a feel to it that he didn't have, then he'll use it. Otherwise, he can complete the entire work without saying a word to anybody. It's convenience: you can do it all by yourself, all hours of the day and night."

Even though Prince had assembled the Revolution as a live band by this point, in the studio, he was still very much the captain of his own ship, offering an example of why via a time "when it was three o'clock in the morning, and I'd try to get Bobby Z to come out to the studio, some-times he'd come, sometimes he wouldn't." Expanding more in-depthly on his preference for recording as a one-man band, Prince explained that out-of-necessity "that whole thing came from my early days, when I was working with a lot of people who weren't exactly designed for their jobs...I had to do a lot, and I had to have control, because a lot of them didn't know exactly what was needed... My music wants to do what it wants to do, and I just want to get out of its way...This is my job. This (soundboard) is my desk." Confirming Prince was in the captain's chair for the majority of the album's recording, keyboardist Matt 'Dr.' Fink recalled that "on *1999*, it was all him other than bringing Lisa in to do some vocals, and there was some stuff that Dez did, but it was mainly a Prince solo project in the studio."

Revealing more detail on why he often found himself a slave to his talent, Prince began by explaining that, quite involuntarily, "even if the music was coming through me, I was still listening to it as an admirer of the sound, so whatever I heard, be it a lyric or a melody line or a beat or whatever, sometimes just the bass line, I paid attention to it, and I would let that start the song first. Once you get that main thing down, then that's the leader and that's gonna tell you what the next instrument is supposed to be...(With) my music...I never slow down. I'm constantly occupied with music...when people say I make too many records, I just show them the Aretha Franklin catalogue in the '60s, when she made a new record every four months...I like to go with my intuition. Something hits me and I need to get the track down before I can move on. It's like there's another person inside me, talking to me, and I'm learning to listen to that voice... I feel that music is a blessing. I don't feel like I'm working. So when I'm not 'working,' I'm thinking about it, so music takes up a good portion of the time." Expanding further, Prince explained that when a song idea seizes ahold of him, "sometimes it is a curse, but it's also a blessing. It's a gift that I am completely grateful for. That's why I keep (making music), because I don't want to be ungrateful for the gift."

Sharing fans even further insight into his songwriting process for *1999*, Prince next explained that "I try to let the song dictate its own direction... it is different all the time. The main way that something comes is fully completed. And the fun part is just listening. When I'm writing, sometimes the pen just goes. I'm not in charge and I'm almost listening outside of it...I seldom wrote at any instruments. But I'm definitely into letting sounds dictate...not the way I write a song, but the way I develop my ideas…I write in my head. The rest is just dictation." While Prince might have simplified his recording process down to something as simple as *dictation*, engineer Peggy McCreary, who recorded portions of *1999* alongside Prince at Sunset Sound, offered a contrasting and more realistic opinion of the artist's recording process wherein "he doesn't make records like other people. He doesn't have any set hours and he doesn't have a set way of doing things. Nothing is normal." Elaborating further on the latter, fellow Sunset Sound engineer David Leonard revealed that it was not uncommon during the recording of 1999 for Prince to "go into the studio with a song in his mind, record it, overdub it, sing it and mix it all in one shot, start to finish."

Offering the album's title track as a specific example of the latter process in action, Sunset Sound assistant engineer Peter Doell recalled that "one of the guys I worked with was insanely talented—he was called Prince. When he first showed up, he was in all-purple and no one could figure out what the heck he was up to. A guy called David Leonard and his wife Peggy used to do his sessions and I got to work on a couple. The guy was so incredibly creative. I remember days when Prince would come into the studio at like 9am, kick you out of the room for about twenty minutes, then he'd write a song —'*1999*' was a day like that. Then he'd come back into the (recording) room and you'd better have the drums tuned up and ready because he's going to play the daylights out of the drums—he was an incredible drummer. Then he'd go on and do the bass, keyboards and by one o'clock you're mixing it and by four o'clock you run off and have it mastered. So from nine-to-five, you went from not having even written the song to having it mastered. He was an unbelievable cottage industry." Picking up on the momentum the latter engineer described as Prince's norm during the writing/recording of *1999*, mainstay engineer Peggy McCreary explained that "I felt this was his best time…He was so prolific. He was just so on and had so much coming out of him." Prince for his own part would concede in hindsight that the album's length was out of his hands, offering years later that "I didn't want to do a double record, but I just kept on writing."

Describing how Prince's super-human work ethic could at times collide with the realities of mortal fatigue on the part of his engineers, Peggy

McCreary recalled that "some of the songs were so long and he couldn't quit. He just kept going and going and going. And that was so hard, because then you had to overdub them. A long song meant a long day and that is how he would wear you down. He needs his sleep but only after a certain point. I've read that it's characteristic of geniuses: they go for long periods of time without sleep and then they go for days with nothing but sleep. It was funny because I'd ask him, 'Are you hungry?' He'd say, 'You stop trying to feed me, because that makes me sleepy.'… Sometimes I was yawning and was so tired, and Prince would just look at me and say 'Just set me up and you can get out of here for a while.' But he wouldn't let you go home. I remember setting him up a microphone above the mixing board and giving him a pair of headphones so he could monitor what he was singing. And he would run the machine and he'd just sing like crazy. It was four in the morning and I'd hear this 'waaahh' and stomping coming from the control room…I remember one day when…he really came in with an attitude and sat down at the drums and told me to put up clean tape. I had been told that we would be mixing so I had very quickly to re-patch the board, tear it all down to set up everything and mic it for recording. You had to be really fast. Meanwhile, he would be playing drums and say 'Come on Peggy, you're blowing the groove, you're losing me here.' The pressure was incredible… He had no tolerance for human weakness."

When not recording in L.A. at Sunset Sound, Prince worked at his home studio recording over the summer of 1982, with keyboardist Matt 'Dr.' Fink recalling that "Prince recorded a lot of the *1999* album in the same home studio he did *Purple Rain* in, though he hadn't painted the house purple yet, and the studio set-up was built into the basement, with a Soundcraft console, and an MCI 24-track machine. He had big Westlake monitors mounted on the wall, and there was an isolation room, so he'd had some construction done on that particular home studio to make it more viable as an acoustic-engineered room. He had a drum set and every keyboard of the day—the Oberheim and the Omni, which was a very integral keyboard used on *1999*. His guitar rigs were Boogie Amps, and he had Fenders and Marshalls and various other amps, and his outboard gear included all the state-of-the-art equipment of the day, which would have included the Lexicon 224 reverbs, the Lexicon digital delays of that time, the Eventide outboard equipment, and the latest AMS RMX-16 digital reverb, the same one Phil Collins used on '*In the Air Tonight.*'"

Of the album's drum-machine and synthesizer-heavy presence, Prince recalled that "I've had this Roger Linn drum machine since 1981. It's one of the first drum machines ever created. It takes me five seconds to put together a beat on this thing. So from the very start, technology gave me a direct result for my efforts… I *can* do all the programming myself. *1999* is nothing but me running all the computers myself… Technology used to play a big part in my music." From a band-member's perspective on Prince's decision to record so much of *1999* by himself at his home studio, drummer Bobby Z recalled that "I felt like an auto assembley worker looking at a robot for the first time, wondering if I had a job. It was so early for drum machines, I didn't know what to make of it. It certainly kept good time.'" Expanding in detail on why Prince so favored the Linn drum machines in the course of the album's recording, Dr. Fink explained that "the Linn LM1, in those days, Prince used the Linn because (A) It was the fattest-sounding machine out, and (B) It was one of the few available at the time. The only other machine was the Roland DMX series, which I believe he used a little bit on the *1999* album, I know he had one around, but we never had it on stage, but the Linn was what he preferred because it was beefier, chunkier, very unique sounding, and really one of the very first truly professional-sounding drum machines. That was the reason why that one was kept around and used on *1999*, and all the way through the Purple Rain era and beyond. Even though there were the Linn 2 and then Linn 9000, the changes came to those other machines, they didn't sound the same, which is why he never messed with them. So the LM1 was the basis for a lot of those earlier hits." Expanding further, maintenance tech Don Batts offered his observation that 'I think innovation was the key for him when he was working with the drum machine."

Of the album's other dominant instrument, which *Rolling Stone Magazine* called "artfully arranged synthesizer pop," and *Billboard Magazine* noted was "constructed almost entirely on synthesizers by Prince himself," keyboardist Matt 'Dr.' Fink began by explaining that "the Omni keyboard was very heavily used on *1999*, much like the song *Dirty Mind*, so that synthesizer—besides the Oberheims—was integral throughout *Dirty Mind* through *1999*, and in particular on that title track. *Little Red Corvette* was Oberheim heavy, strictly Oberheim, and '*DanceMusicSexRomance*' and '*Let's Pretend We're Married*' were also both heavy Oberheim. But *1999* was strictly the Omni 2. With the new Omni, they didn't change the aspects of the Omni in the sense of what it did originally, which was combine the old ARP string machine—which had first debuted on the song '*Dreamweaver*' by Gary Wright—that was one of the first original ARP string synthesizers, which is strictly a string machine. Then what they did was take a lot of that same sound, improve upon it, then put it into the Omni, and added that synthesizer section to it, so you could blend the two. So that was the original ARP Omni, and then the second ARP Omni, the Omni 2, was introduced, with control enhancements and button changes, and they had improved on the sound, the controls, but basically it did the same thing. But it sounded different from the Oberheim, and so *1999* in particular, that was the main instrument."

Continuing, Fink further recalled that "what was happening at that time is that any technically new keyboard that came out that specific year he would get it, we would get all the gear that was available to make sounds with, and would always be on the cutting edge of that being a Warners' act, and having the equipment budgets plus the royalties Prince got from previous projects, he invested that for the most part back into music equipment. He would come to me and Lisa from time to time and ask us 'Hey, what's new and hot on the market,' because he wasn't always keeping up with keyboards. And we'd say 'Well, we want this, and we should get that,' and one day I told him 'We need to get the new version of the Omni; they've improved it and enhanced the workings of it, and it sounds better;' so he purchased those, and at that same time, the OBX-A's came in, which was the next version from the Oberheim OBX, so that was played on the record too."

In terms of which songs Prince chose to share record air-time with as *1999* developed, Dr. Fink recalled that "on that album, sometimes he would work the song out with the band as he was writing it, and start teaching us the song, and then he would go back in the studio and finish it. Or in other cases, he would just go in and do them, and then present them to us on a tape when it was finished, and I'd say 80% of the time, that's how it was done. Whereafter he'd hand us a cassette of the mixed song, say 'Okay, go learn this and we'll start rehearsing it.' " Of the collaborative vocal recording on *1999*, Dr. Fink recalled that "in the beginning of *1999*, that was all his voice being run through a harmonizer tuned way down…he also brought Lisa and Dez in to sing on *Little Red Corvette*." Keyboardist Lisa Coleman recalled that the literal inspiration for the hit came when "I bought this vintage pink Mercury at a car auction…It was so bitching-looking that Prince used to borrow it and dent it, which I'd make him feel bad about. He slept in it one time and came up with *Little Red Corvette*…even though it was a pink Mercury." Elaborating on his participation on the latter hit single, guitarist Dez Dickerson revealed that, during the song's tracking, "it was just Prince and I in his home studio when we recorded it. He played me the track once, and then we started tracking. He would always let me play what I wanted to (I appreciate the fact that he 'trusted' my playing). I recorded three different versions of the solo, and he later 'comped' them into one, using different sections of all three. I was finished within half an hour!"

Once principle tracking had concluded, principle sound engineer Peggy McCreary recalled that during mixing, "it was a hell of a lot of work… There were a lot of cross fades and hours and hours of editing. I had six 2-track machines going and it was just a mess." Looking back on a more positive note in retrospect one of her favorite nights during recording, McCreary cited an album B-Side and live fan favorite for years, '*How Come You Don't Call Me Anymore*,' explaining that "that "Studio 2 at Sunset Sound had a great piano, and if you listen to the song, you can hear his feet on the pedals. He was in a really good mood that night and he made that evening so fun. That was one of our best nights. He had such a soulful way of singing and it really shows. The song fades a few seconds too early because he goes on for a little bit longer."

Released on October 27th, 1982, *1999* would mark Prince's commercial break-through, becoming his first Billboard Top 10 Album debut (#9), and inspiring *Rolling Stone Magazine* to conclude that "*1999* may be Prince's most influential album: Its synth-and-drum machine-heavy arrangements codified the 'Minneapolis sound' that loomed over mid-'80s R&B and pop, not to mention the next two decades' worth of electro, house, and techno… on *1999*, a double album of extended dance pieces, it featured his best song, '*Little Red Corvette*,' and an example of his musical wit, '*1999*." Spawning 3 Top 20 hits, including two top 10 smashed with the aforementioned '*Little Red Corvette*' (#6) and '*Delirious*' (#8), along with the album's title track (# 12), with 1999, according to *Billboard Magazine*, Prince had "constructed an album dominated by computer funk, but he didn't simply rely on the extended instrumental grooves to carry the album—he didn't have to when his songwriting was improving by leaps and bounds…the result is a stunning display of raw talent." For Prince, the commercial break-through seemed like a welcome reward for the tireless work he'd put in over the four years and previous studio albums building to the point where the singer finally made "the cover of *Rolling Stone*," quipping in the same commentary that "it took me four albums."

'In some ways Purple Rain scared me…
It's my albatross and it'll be hanging around
my neck as long as I'm making music.'

—Prince, 1985

Chapter 13:

*Purple Rain—*1984

By 1983, with the break-out success of *1999*, Prince had become a bonafide rock idol, but was still a few million albums short of the super-stardom he'd dreamed of since his teens. With his sights fixed on international chart dominance and beyond, former manager Bob Cavallo recalling at the time "he had a clear vision—he was vitally interested in music, but also in success…That's an incredibly powerful combination, someone who wants to be successful but who will not sacrifice quality of musical vision." For Prince, that vision had expanded from record stores to movie houses, based around a concept Prince had been drafting in his head for years for a semi-biopic film entitled '*Purple Rain*,' with keyboardist Lisa Coleman explaining that "when I first joined back in the days of *Dirty Mind*, he was already talking about his ideas for what would be *Purple Rain*," while Drummer Bobby Z added that "the movie was talked about for a long time…He was always talking about doing a movie." Demonstrating just how serious he was about getting the project launched, Prince—whose managerial contract was due to expire in the summer of 1983—hinged his willingness to resign to managers' Bob Cavallo and Steve Fargnoli's ability to secure financing for the project. Steve Fargnoli reportedly relayed a conversation to partner Cavallo at the time wherein Prince's instructions were "simple…He wants a movie. If we don't get him a deal with a major studio, he won't stay with us."

While Cavallo, Ruffalo and Fargnoli began hunting around for a film studio to partner with, initial production on the film began with a $4 million investment from Warner Bros. Records head Mo Ostin, with Revolution keyboardist Matt 'Dr.' Fink recalling that "I remember my reaction when Prince first announced we were going to do a movie, which was towards the end of the *1999* tour, and he had joined me for lunch one day at one of the hotels, and just sat down and discussed the whole movie thing for me, and I thought the whole thing sounded very exciting. He never would belie any fear or trepidation or uncertainty about the whole thing, he was very confident about it. And Warners was uncertain at first about putting Prince in a movie at that stage of his career, they thought 'He sold 2 or 3 million copies of *1999*, and has come a long way since we signed him,' but they were scared they were going to lose their shirts making the movie. So in the end, Prince's management believed in it so much that they started out investing their own money into the movie to get the production off the ground. They managed to do some sort of loan scenario from Warners, and they ended up fronting some of the money along with Bob Cavallo, one of Prince's managers. So they barely got that thing going, and it was touch and go this whole time leading up to when we moved into the *Purple Rain*-era warehouse in the summer of 1983."

Continuing, Fink explained that "each tour had a different place to rehearse, so Prince was renting different spaces at different times, so the particular warehouse where we rehearsed and worked out the *Purple Rain* songs, and recorded some of it was a building in St. Louis Park, which was actually the suburb I grew up in, literally half a mile from the high school I attended. It was situated off of Highway 7, about 10 minutes from downtown Minneapolis, and was just a building that had been used for some other business, and so Prince just plunked a basic stage in there, and the soundboard, and a 24-track machine and some outboard gear and effects—which included some gating units for gating stuff, Teletronics compressors, some API outboard EQ, JML mic-pre amps, some Lexicon reverbs like the 224, the Lexicon digital delay, some Eventide harmonizers in the rack for vocals, to give it that kind of doubling-chorus kind of vibe. It was a pretty good sized building. The mixing console at the warehouse was a really kind of basic upper-end Soundcraft, which was mainly used for tracking, then Prince mixed later in L.A. on some really high-end Neve at Sunset Sound." Elaborating further, drummer Bobby Z recalled that "Prince put the board in the middle of this huge, echoey place…That gave all the tracks a live feel."

Elaborating on the Warehouse's recording set-up, engineer David Leonard recalled that "in trying to set up a mini-recording studio in this warehouse, I asked first if there was a mobile recording truck available, and there was none, but it just so happened that Westlake Audio was trying to sell Prince an API Console, and had had it shipped to Minneapolis in a crate. And he'd looked at it and I guess somebody had sharpied on the knobs and I think he didn't like that, so it was still sitting in the crate—presumably waiting to be returned. So I decided to use that, and told him I needed to set up that night and we could do it the next day. So we took that API Console out of the crate and set it up on road cases, and I had fed-exed from L.A. a bunch of XLR-to-TRF adaptor patch cables, and just ran it off the end of the P.A. snake and went into the patch points on the patch bay."

After rehearsing for the majority of the summer of 1983 in the St. Louis Park Warehouse, the band debuted roughly half of what would become the *Purple Rain* soundtrack at a Charity Benefit at the First Avenue nightclub on August 3rd, 1983. At the concert, Prince debuted the newest addition to his newly-christened live band The Revolution, rhythm guitarist/backing vocalist Wendy Melvoin, life-long friend of keyboardist Lisa Coleman. Recalling the sequence of events which led to Melvoin's joining the group, keyboardist Matt Dr. Fink explained that "Wendy wasn't brought into the band until just before the filming of *Purple Rain*, when Dez quit, and it was a real sort-of emergency replacement thing, and originally Prince had wanted Dez to be in the movie, and ended up featuring him in a cameo singing '*Modernaire*.'

So when Wendy came aboard, she had already kind of been jamming with us from being Lisa's best friend, even when Dez was around, and so one day Prince just announced 'Wendy's joining the group,' and Wendy played on all of those live recordings. It was a pretty smooth transition, there were some moments when she was technically challenged—like the solo on '*When Doves Cry*,' Prince had wanted her to play that live instead of him having to, so that definitely presented more of a challenge for her, I felt, but she really worked hard and learned it and got around it. I thought she was a great player, she was very young and still learning, and things gelled within the band as time went on." Elaborating on the audition process, bandmate Lisa Coleman recalled that one day when Dez Dickerson failed to show up at a band rehearsal, Melvoin sat in for him at sound check, explaining that "Wendy free-formed on an acoustic and Prince was blown away...Then the 'Funky Little Wendy' side of her came out and it was just over, Prince began a love affair with her playing."

In a reflection of just how confident Prince felt about Wendy's fitting into and rounding out his new band's sound, maintenance tech and future engineer Susan Rogers felt from her own observations that "she came furthest of anyone I've ever seen at pulling Prince out of his shell. He adored her and felt comfortable with her. Everyone else was more or less intimidated by him." For her own part, Wendy explained reciprocally that "Prince gave me a lot of encouragement on breaking my own limitations. I didn't know about being in a band. He gave me the strength to understand what my gift was." From her earliest days as a member of the Revolution, drummer Bobby Z further recalled that Wendy fit into the group—beyond a musical vantage point—because "she had the hunger. Matt and I still had the hunger, and Mark certainly had the hunger. Wendy was just at the absolute right place at the right time...It was more fun to be together with Wendy in the band. We'd hang out more and we rehearsed more and got more done as a band because we liked each other better. It was easier for Prince to work with us. Wendy learned extremely quick, which is what you had to do. Her personality brought so much to balance the band out and make it the band it became. It couldn't have become the Revolution with Dez. It needed Wendy to bring out that extra oomph!"

Including '*Baby I'm a Star*,' '*Computer Blue*,' and the album's title track, '*Purple Rain*,' former road manager Alan Leeds recalled of that night's success at First Avenue that while "it was hot and humid…Purple Rain brought the house down. That's the version on the album. Thank God we got it on tape." Technically-speaking, engineer David Leonard, who recorded the show alongside fellow engineer David Z, recalled that "I was using a mobile recording studio truck on loan from the Record Plant, which had an API console built into the truck, and Ampex. We hadn't rehearsed for that show with Prince, so I just flew in from L.A. and headed to First Avenue to record the concert, and when you're recording live, you just make sure you're getting level, and we weren't actually mixing it live, I was just trying to get it on tape live." Elaborating further, keyboardist Matt 'Dr.' Fink explained that "when we performed at First Avenue to debut the music, the actual song *Purple Rain* was tracked live in the early fall of 1983, just before we started to film the movie. We'd already been rehearsing a lot of the material for the movie, and they brought in a live recording truck to track the basic tracks, and then later Prince did some more overdubbing on those basic tracks. For *Purple Rain*, we'd rehearsed it a lot and pretty much knocked it out in one take for the show."

Recounting the creative origins of '*Purple Rain*' prior to its live debut, Fink explained that "*Purple Rain* was just a work in progress when Prince came in with it one day to rehearsal, with the chord progression and most of the lyrics done. He had the melody and the lyric, but he was still tweaking it when he came to the band to work out the rhythm parts. So it was worked out with the band in the warehouse, Prince had come in with the chordal progression on guitar, and they said 'Let's jam on this, and each of you come up with your own parts.' We jammed on it for about 2 hours, running through the chord progression with him singing, and Prince first played it on guitar, and then I joined in on piano, then Lisa on guitar, and Bobby started running the groove based on Prince's tempo on the guitar, and Mark on bass. The string arrangement was done after the fact on an overdub by Clare Fisher, and we recreated it live by using the Oberheims for the strings. If you listen to the end of Purple Rain where he sings that big falsetto line, that came from the jam session from a line that I was playing on the upper register of the piano, based on his chord progression. We were just playing instrumentally at that point, he wasn't singing off the song, and then he latched onto that, heard me playing and started singing the falsetto part, and ended up adopting it for the whole end-piece at the end of the song. Once that jam session was done, that's pretty much how you hear it on the record. So that song was something of a group effort." Upon its release, *Billboard Magazine* would hail the title track as "a majestic ballad filled with brilliant guitar flourishes."

When attention turned to another of the record's smash hits, '*I Would Die For You,*' Fink recalled that "that song he really worked out himself in the home studio, and then brought to the band prior to the First Avenue live show that was recorded. I remember when it came time to learn it, initially, he wanted me or Lisa to play that pulsing bass part with like two fingers kind of playing one note, and you from what I understand, he played that in the studio live in time like that. That's like Liberace or Billy Joel, and was very technically difficult to perform. So I tried doing that live at rehearsal, which I was able to do, and Lisa was handling the main chords, and so Prince then came to me and asked 'Can you play that pulsing rhythm with one hand and play the chords with your left?' And I said, 'I can certainly try!' And it just proved too difficult for me. That was something technically that was too hard, so he said 'Well, I really need you to fatten it up with the chords and have that pulsing bass going.' So I said 'I have an idea: how would you feel about using a sequencer to do that?' And it wasn't something he'd done before, and wasn't totally adverse to it, but asked me 'How are you going to achieve it?' And I had just purchased a Memory Moog Plus for myself to actually use on tour, I used to play the solo from '*When Doves Cry*' on that machine as well, although the original was done by Prince on the Oberheim, I used the Memory Moog for it live because it made it sound better than the Oberheim, in my opinion. It had a little bit better vibe, and I actually prefer the Moog oscillator to the others, and the Memory Moog Plus had a sequencer on board, and MIDI, which early in those days was called the Musical Instrument Digital Interface, which allowed you to take a cable from one synthesizer, connect it to another, and trigger that machine from the other. So you could layer synthesizers, and have the Memory Moog Plus triggering a Yamaha

DX7, if you wanted a fatter sound, or two different sounds layered. So Prince was using the Linn LM1 drum machine in those days, which was the first truly programmable drum machine of the day. They came out in 1980 and 1981, and Prince had started using it almost immediately on Controversy, and he still had those around. There wasn't a Midi-version of the Linn LM1 yet, so I went to Don Batts, who was Prince's all-around tech guy, with the dilemma of 'How can we make the bass and the Linn work together?' Because the Linn was the drum machine used on '*I Would Die for You*,' and Don said 'Well, I have to build a modified Midi interface for the Linn, and customize it,' and he did, and basically built a mini-interface that would lock up to the sequencer on the Memory Moog. And he basically made it so that the Memory Moog became a slave to the Linn, through Midi, so that when Bobby pushed the play button on the Linn, it would trigger the Memory Moog, and the Memory Moog synthesizer had the bass part step-recorded into it, and it worked! So basically Don Batts did a completely innovative, new thing that had never been done before with a Linn machine triggering the Memory Moog on that song live, and I'd say about 98% of the time, it worked flawlessly." Continuing, engineer David Leonard recalled that "*I Would Die for You*' began as a live track that we later worked on overdubs in the studio, that was one where we triggered synths and stuff off of the tracks."

Of the album/film's opening track, '*Let's Go Crazy*,' engineer David Leonard revealed that the smash hit "was recorded in a warehouse out-side of Minneapolis. At the time, I would fly back and forth from L.A. to Minneapolis as Prince was shooting *Purple Rain*, so I'd come in to town to work in the studio in the basement of his house in Chanhassen generally, because this was before Paisley Park was around. In that studio, he had a Soundcraft Console. I would generally work with him at night because he'd be working on the movie during the day, and I know we would work over there a little bit, but on the weekend I recorded '*Let's Go Crazy*,' Prince wanted me to go to the warehouse where he rehearsed, and he had the full-on production rehearsal with lights and sound, and they were working on that song and wanted to record it. It's almost like it was supposed to be done the night of the show, but we were recording it after the fact. I don't know if he wrote it later, or what the case was, but that was the order. I remember we went to some radio station in St. Paul and got a pair of Uri monitors off the wall, and put those up, but still, the band had a P.A. blasting and I was in the corner of a warehouse, so I had to use headphones to record. The drums on that song were 2 sets of LM1 Lynn drums that Prince had Bobby playing pads on the triggers that were triggering the Lynn drums, and then there was also a loop running, so the only mics I had on the kit were hat and the overheads. For the guitars—we miced the stacks. The band had rehearsed it, so we just rolled tape and went. It wasn't more than one or two takes, and it was done. So that's how we recorded '*Let's Go Crazy*'. It was my favorite song I recorded with him because I recorded it on a shoe-string on a console with a pair of headphones, he had some amazing material."

Elaborating further, keyboardist Matt Fink recalled that, compositionally, "*Let's Go Crazy*' was a song Prince came to the band with, but we recorded the rhythm section with him live. He taught it to us in rehearsal one day. He taught that organ intro to me on the Oberheim, and I played that live for the recording. It was a Parfeza organ sound, like an old garage band organ, an old-style box organ, it was very similar tonally to that." Continuing, engineer David Leonard explained that following principle tracking at the warehouse, "we did some overdubs there, but afterward, we took it back to Sunset Sound and Prince did vocal and guitar overdubs, from that warehouse recording, and then we mixed it like the rest of the record in L.A."

With almost half of the soundtrack recorded in the course of the First Avenue charity benefit concert, engineer David Leonard next detailed the rest of the album's progression as one wherein "because we recorded the show live first, that was one entity, Purple Rain started when we recorded the tracks of the live show at First Avenue, it was the same time that the Time played and Vanity 6, so it was like in the movie, really the same show. The Time's record, Ice Cream Castles, came out of that show, and '*America*', '*Jungle Love,*' and '*The Bird*', that was all from the same night that Purple Rain's live tracks were recorded. Those included '*Purple Rain,*' '*Computer Blue,*' and '*I Would Die for You,*' so the live recordings that ended up on that record were really from the First Avenue club, except those we did back in the studio. Then as Prince started writing and filming the movie, and the other songs he wrote to fit into scenes from the movie, so the soundtrack was very much built around the movie. We spent more time on that record than any other record—for instance, I think we did Shelia E's *'Glamorous Life'* record in 11 days—and the Time's record went really fast—but we spent months and months on *Purple Rain.* Because we recorded around the filming, new material would come up depending on what he was writing for the movie."

When in Minneapolis not rehearsing or recording at the St. Louis Park Warehouse, Prince could often be found working at his home studio at the legendary-amongst-fans purple house, which keyboardist Matt 'Dr.' Fink recalled "wasn't originally purple, it was an existing white stucco house out in Chanhassen, with brown and wood trim, Mediterranean-style and he had the stucco painted purple. His studio set-up at that house was built into the basement, he had big Westlake monitors mounted up in the wall, and there was an isolation room, so he'd had some construction done on that particular home studio to make it more viable as an acoustic-engineered room. He again had the same type of board that was used to track Purple Rain, the Soundcraft console. They were using the old MCI 24-track machine. He had a drum set and every keyboard of the day—the Oberheim and the Omni, which was a very integral keyboard used on 1999. He didn't use it much on Purple Rain, but was really using the Oberheims quite a bit on the Purple Rain album. His guitar rigs were Boogie Amps, and he had Fenders and Marshalls and various other amps, so he had a variety of tonal quality, and on Purple Rain, he was using the Chuck Orr guitars, which he used on the record, in the movie, and on tour so it would match up sound-wise." Recalling further Prince's recording preferences during this period, newly hired maintenance tech and future sound engineer Susan Rogers explained that "There was a basic sound during the years I worked for him. He liked the drums, the bass, the vocals a certain way—there were only two microphones he would use for his vocals…When Prince recorded his vocals, he wanted complete privacy…So I'd set up a vocal mic right in the control room, set up a tape machine so he had tracks to record on, he'd be all ready to go, and then everyone would leave the room and he would do the vocals by himself. He would come out and get us when he was done."

Following completion of the live portion of the album's tracking, recording moved for five weeks from middle-August through the latter part of September out to Los Angeles and into Studio 3 at Sunset Sound Recording Studios. Working alongside engineers David Leonard and wife Peggy McCreary, McCreary described the layout of Studio 3 as something "like a womb that wrapped around for your protection. We had a bathroom, a kitchen, and we would shut ourselves off from everything." Elaborating on the studio's technical layout, fellow engineer David Leonard explained that "it was all 24-track, Sunset Sound Studio 3 is pretty much where he camped out after 1999, which was done in Studio 2, but once he moved into Studio 3, that became his room for a long time. That studio had an API Frank Diminio Board with API EQ and it had 990 Jenson front-end, and we had a 24-Track on Ampex 456, and never any Simpti or anything, just go. When we got into *Purple Rain*, we weren't locking up tapes, there was still one reel of tape, but on that album, I spent more time messing around with some of the live tracks. Like on '*Computer Blue*', I triggered Synths off of hi-hats and stuff like that. I remember gating stuff and triggering stuff, it was cool." Of the latter track, keyboardist Matt 'Dr.' Fink recalled that "*Computer Blue* originally came out of a jam session one day at the warehouse, and the band was just sort of jamming, and I just started playing this bass part during the jam, which became the main hook-bass on that track, and the band was grooving on that, and Prince latched onto it and built the song around that groove, and came up with the main vocal and hook of that song. Lisa and Wendy also got some writing credits on that song, and Prince worked out the whole transition before it goes to the bridge; and then the main melody is credited to his father, John T. Nelson. It had been hanging out there for quite a while and he incorporated it into the song."

Of Prince's demeanor during the L.A. sessions at Sunset Sound—given the pressure he was under between recording a soundtrack to a film he was simultaneously shooting—Leonard offered that "he was very quiet and very shy when he first came into the studio, when I first saw him, and then after *1999* and then *Purple Rain*, he was a little more comfortable with me. We never got to be friends, like he wouldn't call you up to go hang or anything. He wasn't very happy or friendly, I don't know... he was tortured, I guess that would be the word I'd use. It wasn't that he was unkind, it's just that he was very private and driven. You wouldn't hang out with Prince, he'd call me if he had a song and you'd head over to the studio at 4 O'Clock in the morning, so you'd go down and open the studio so he could record whatever song he'd just written. He's truly a genius-level musician... Everything I saw him do as far as his time and playing on '*Purple Rain*', that was something. I think he always puts himself under musical pressure to make it as genius as he could. Prince doesn't make records like other people...Most people will get a band, cut all their tracks in one week, do overdubs and vocals over the next few months. Then they mix it. Prince will go in, record it, overdub it, sing it and mix it all in one shot. The song never gets off the board. He doesn't leave until it's done. Once, we'd gotten out of the studio at five or six in the morning and he wanted to be back at ten. Sleep is unimportant. He likes coffee. If you ask him to eat, he'll say 'No, it'll make me sleepy.'" Elaborating more in-depthly on Prince's recording pace, engineer Peggy McCreary added that, during these recording sessions, "if I didn't get something done quickly enough, Prince would yell 'I'm losing my groove, Peggy!' " Offering a specific example of the latter in action, McCreary recalled the artist's overdubbing process for string sections on both '*Purple Rain*' and '*Baby I'm a Star*', wherein "he wanted to use strings and all kinds of things. I said 'Excuse me, we only have 24-track machines. We don't have enough room.' And he just said 'Make some more room.' That's just the way he works. So I had to hook up two tape machines."

For those album tracks recorded at Sunset Sound, engineer David Leonard began by explaining that "for Prince's own recordings, unlike say with the Time where the whole band was involved at the studio, Prince was definitely the producer, and on his own material, there definitely were not as many people around—Wendy and Lisa, and Matt Fink sometimes, but not many other than he and I, or whatever engineers were working with him at the time. Honestly, in all those years I recorded with him we never miced the band in the studio or saw them play together live in the studio, I never saw that, it was usually just him. Or if Wendy and Lisa were going to play something, like a piano part, they'd be there. Lisa played piano sometimes, and Shelia played some drums, but in my experience, Prince was playing most of that stuff, he played it all. I never really saw a lot of the band in the studio, Prince was playing a lot of his own instrumentation on that record, and Shelia E was playing a lot of the drum tracks too during recording. Prince and Shelia were friends, and I think they had a genuine affinity for each other, and their drumming styles. She was around a lot, and she even played some of the drums on the *Purple Rain* album. Prince played A LOT of everything you hear on *Purple Rain* in the studio, and Wendy and Lisa were around a lot, and Shelia E, but that was pretty much it."

When recording Prince's drum tracks for album tracks like '*Take Me With U*' among others, Leonard explained that "as the recording for Purple Rain came around, Prince was using a lot more live drums. The most impressive thing about working with Prince in the studio was his internal clock, it was amazing, his time. For instance, when he was playing drums, I've seen him do so without a click track, and stop playing and just keep singing and then come back in playing drums for a breakdown of a song, then be able to come in and pick up an instrument and time it exactly the same over an 8-bar break or something, that's pretty unhuman—*with NO clicktrack*. When we were recording vocals for Purple Rain, Prince liked to use a Lexicon delay often, and that's an effect you hear a lot on his vocals throughout the album."

Songs for the album that Prince recorded during this period included '*The Beautiful Ones*,' which Leonard recalled was "recorded on the Steinway, and I used 414s to mic that piano, it was a scary song, the way he screams. It had a lot of passion and emotion," while another of the album's hit singles, '*Take Me With U*,' Leonard explained, "was done as a studio track, and he played Oberheim keyboards on that, and I tracked some of Appalonia's vocals for that song, which went alright. She could sing, and what I remember more than anything with her was actually recording her on a demo for '*Manic Monday*', which Prince wrote for the Bangles. It was originally a Prince track, which he sang first, then she sang along with him." Offering a contrasting opinion to Leonard's regarding Appalonia's vocal abilities, future Prince engineer and primary maintenance tech at the time Susan Rogers—who was present at the L.A. Sessions—for her part, recalled that "Apollonia couldn't sing... The day we had to record '*Take Me With U*', Prince brought her...to rehearse. When recording vocals with other singers, there would be just him, as producer and engineer, and the singer, usually sitting in the booth in the dark. I remember thinking, this is gonna be a long night. He coaxed her into being more assertive. He has an incredible talent for recognizing strengths and weaknesses. He has marvelous leadership, is very good at knowing just how to push you to get the best out of you, and he knew when to stop, in most cases. '*Take Me With U*' was perfect." Elaborating further on Prince's micro-managerial process for mapping out vocal parts, Revolution guitarist/backing vocalist Wendy Melvoin revealed that "Prince would put down guidelines for vocals. He did that every time. You had to copy every lick, every breath, every sigh, no question, especially with his ghost bands. They had to follow everything he did, precisely."

While Prince had finished out the summer, recording additional mate-rial for the soundtrack in Los Angeles, back in Minneapolis Revolution keyboardist Matt 'Dr.' Fink recalled that "Prince's managers had hired an acting coach for the whole summer of 1983, and the whole band was holed up in this building for 3 months straight, and a couple of times a week, we had an acting tutor we worked with. Then in downtown Minneapolis, there was this dance school, and we had to go through dancing lessons—it was mandatory at first, but Prince loosened up after a while with the band. I went there for every class, and did it to pretty much stay in shape, he would do the Jane Fonda workout and some Broadway style dance moves, and some days it would be just me and the girls from Vanity 6. But we had to do the acting classes, and they weren't even working on the script yet, we were just doing acting exercises, and memory games." With filming wrapping as the fall went on, the soundtrack was largely completed, sans what would become arguably its biggest hit, the famously bass-less '*When Doves Cry*,' with engineer Peggy McCreary recalling that "he came in, cut it and mixed it in a day. He was listening to it playing back, and just popped the bass out." Elaborating more indepthly, engineer David Leonard added that "*When Doves Cry*' was a studio track done in L.A. at Sunset Sound, and I remember it had A LOT of stuff on it, so when it came down to mixing the song, it originally had bass on it, and he made the decision to remove the bass. I was originally trying to mix it as it was, but he came in and turned it off, and put reverb on the bass drum and away you go." Prince, for his part, explained the decision as one wherein "they were almost done editing the movie…*When Doves Cry* was the last song to be mixed, and it just wasn't sounding right…It was just sounding too conventional, like every other song with drums and bass and keyboards. So I said, 'If I could have it my way it would sound like this,' and I pulled the bass out of the mix…Sometimes your brain kind of splits in two—your ego tells you one thing, and the rest of you says something else. You have to go with what you know is right." *Billboard Magazine*, for one, agreed, concluding that "the bass-less '*When Doves Cry*' is an eerie, spare neo-psychedelic masterpiece."

Of another of the album's last-minute additions, '*Darling Nikki*,' arguably the album's most provocative song, engineer David Leonard recalled the track as one "Prince recorded in his basement in Minneapolis, you can tell the sound of that one is pretty different. He brought it in as is, mixed." Prince, for his part, felt looking back on the controversial song's addition to the soundtrack that "when I was making sexy tunes, that wasn't all I was doing. Back then, the sexiest thing on TV was 'Dynasty,' and if you watch it now, it's like 'The Brady Bunch.' My song 'Darling Nikki' was considered porn because I said the word masturbate. Tipper Gore got so mad…It's so funny now." Keyboardist Matt 'Dr.' Fink, from a band member's point of view, explained that "*Darling Nikki* was another one he did in at his home studio, and when I first heard that one, I thought 'Boy, you've got all these wonderful poppy hit songs all over the album…' and I was a little scared of it at first, in terms of what the reaction would be. I loved the song, but he was obviously trying to push the limits with the song, so it was a little frightening in terms of the subject matter. But I would never have gone to him to protest about it, not that he would have listened to me anyway…I figured he wouldn't have cared, so why bother."

The same absolute autonomy over the project's creative direction extended past recording and into the mixing stages, with engineer Susan Rogers explained that "The production was his alone," while engineer David Leonard recalled a routine in which "when you work for Prince, he was VERY hands-on, I mean you would just set stuff up and he would go and he has a vision, so he would just ask you to do stuff, and if you tried things, he would like it or not, but pretty much he was driving the boat. During that period, mixing norms for Prince involved having the Lexicon reverb on the drums, which involved setting up a chamber and the Lexicon delay, those were the things that were always plugged up. Sunset Sound had 3 actual live chambers, echo rooms with mics in them, and they were set off the mixing board, so when you were mixing, you could run anything through them. So anything Prince mixed during that era out of Sunset Sound, which was all of *1999* and *Purple Rain*, generally had a chamber on it, for all those records."

Continuing, Leonard further elaborated on a broader mixing process of elimination of sorts wherein "when I would edit for him, first of all, every song that we ever recorded was a full reel of tape, like 12—15 minutes long, and everything that came out on the record was edited down to the short, radio versions, but all the originals are long. So the dance versions, the long versions, are the actual originals, they're the full-length versions, and then everything on the record was cut down. So if we were cutting 2-track, I would edit from one verse to a later chorus, and his timing was amazing, he'd tell me cut to this chorus, and point and show me, then I'd mark it on the downbeat and put it together, then he'd say, 'No, make that come in later,' so I'd go back and take like a half-inch piece of tape off of the verse before, then stick it on there, and then he'd say 'Oh no, that's too much, cut that in half,' so then I'd go back and get a half-inch piece of tape and edit it into a quarter-inch piece of tape, and then he'd say 'Okay, cut that in half again,' so now I'm cutting like 8th inch slivers of tape, and he could always tell if I did or didn't do it. His timing was amazing."

Upon completion of the soundtrack's recording, Prince seemed to feel satisfied and calm ahead of the storm of stardom that awaited him, explaining at the time that, regardless of the album's commercial performance, "one thing I'd like to say is that I don't live in a prison. I am not afraid of anything. I haven't built any walls around myself, and I am just like anyone else. I need love and water, and I'm not afraid of a backlash because, like I say, there are people who will support my habits as I have supported theirs. I don't really consider myself a superstar. I live in a small town, and I always will. I can walk around and be me. That's all I want to be, that's all I ever tried to be. I didn't know what was gonna happen. I'm just trying to do my best and if somebody dug it then (cool)." Maintenance technician and future in-house engineer Susan Rogers further recalled that Prince's confidence rooted principally in the fact that "he knew *Purple Rain* was going to be big. He was ecstatic when we finished it."

Released on June 25th, 1984, *Purple Rain* would become the best-selling album of Prince's career, debuting at # 1 on the Billboard Top 200 Album Chart, where it remained for 24 consecutive weeks between August 4th, 1984 and January 18th, 1985, selling in excess of 14 million albums, based on the success of the film's $70 million gross, and the album's four Top 10 singles, including: '*When Doves Cry*' *(# 1)*, '*Let's Go Crazy*' *(# 1)*, '*Purple Rain*' *(# 2)*, and '*I Would Die for You*' *(# 8)*. *Time Magazine*, VH1 and *Rolling Stone Magazine* each ranked the soundtrack as the 15th, 18th, and 72nd Greatest Album of All Time respectively, while Vanity Fair Magazine gave it the distinction of the "Best Soundtrack of All Time", praising the album for its blend of "funk, R&B, pop, metal, and even psychedelia into a sound that defined the '80s." *Entertainment Weekly* declared the album the # 1 on the Top 100 Albums of the past 25 years, while *Billboard Magazine*, for its part, hailed the album's eight tracks as "among his finest songs…Prince's songwriting is at its peak…Taken together, all of the stylistic experiments add up to a stunning statement of purpose that remains one of the most exciting rock & roll albums ever recorded." The Miami Herald celebrated the fact that "every song stands strongly on its own as another majestic offering from the Prince." *Rolling Stone Magazine*, meanwhile, paid Prince perhaps his highest compliment, placing him on the proverbial throne of rock superstardom with their conclusion that with the musical and commercial accomplishment of *Purple Rain*, "Prince seems to have tapped into some extraterrestrial musical dimension where black and white styles are merely different aspects of the same funky thing. Prince's rock & roll is as authentic and compelling as his soul and his extremism is endearing in an era of play-it-safe record production and formulaic hit mongering. *Purple Rain* (is)...loaded with life and invention and pure rock & roll thunder... (Like) Jimi and Sly, Prince writes his own rules. Some of his effects are singularly striking—and his vocals continue to be among the most adventurous and accomplished on the current scene. Prince also does wonderful things with string-section sounds...Anyone partial to great creators should own this record. Like Jimi and Sly, Prince is an original; but apart from that, he's like no one else." Ultimately, Prince made his bones commercially and critically with Purple Rain, garnering three Grammy Awards for Best Rock Vocal Performance by a Duo or Group, Best Album of Original Score Written for a Motion Picture or TV Special (*Purple Rain*), and Best R&B Song, and a nomination for Album of the Year, as well as winning an Oscar for Best Original Song Score in 1985. Heading into the future, Prince's potential was both artistically and commercially boundless, as was his ambition to push his sonic universe even more deeply outward into the unknown than arguably any mainstream recording artist had gone since the Beatles and Brian Wilson in the 1960s... With *Purple Rain*, Prince had sparked his own musical revolution.

"We looked around and I knew we were lost...
There was no place to go but down. You can never
satisfy the need after (the success of Purple Rain)."

—Prince in 1985

Chapter 14:

Around the World in a Day—
1985

As successful as the *Purple Rain* phenomenon had been commercially, grossing over $70 million at the Box Office, selling over 12 million copies, and drawing 1.75 million people over the course of his $30 million grossing world concert tour, Prince, according to tour manager Alan Leeds, by the tour's conclusion, had developed "fears of being typecast as Mr. *Purple Rain*...By the time that tour was over, he was so sick of that music and that whole concept...He was determined to give people another image." Seeking to head musically in an entirely different direction, Prince would soon thereafter deliver his first true art-rock album with *Around the World in a Day*, which drummer Bobby Z recalled, preceding its release the singer "just couldn't wait to get...out." Elaborating further, Revolution keyboardist Matt 'Dr.' Fink recalled that "it was one of those records like *1999*, where he had sat down with us when he decided to end the *Purple Rain* tour, and told us all to take a break and that we weren't doing anything for two years. He told us we'd all be on retainer, and could do solo albums or do whatever we wanted with our lives at that point, and then basically went into the studio, and within four months, delivered the record."

Still, following the conclusion of the Purple Rain tour, Prince had initially told fans "I have to go now. I don't know when I'll be back." Of course, where he went was right from the stage into the studio, explaining for his own part in the aftermath of *Purple Rain's* massive success that "in some ways, that was more detrimental than good...People's perception of me changed after that, and it pigeonholed me. I saw kids coming to concerts who screamed just because that's where the audience screamed in the movie. That's why I did *'Around the World in a Day,'* to totally change that. I wanted not to be pigeonholed." Elaborating further on what changes he was seeking musically to make with *Around the World in a Day*, Prince reasoned that "real music lovers appreciate innovation. Real music lovers have heard everything, so you have to surprise them. Real music lovers need constant stimulation...It just gets more and more interesting every day. More than anything else, I try not to repeat myself. It's the hardest thing in the world to do—there's only so many notes one human being can muster. I write a lot more than people think I do, and I try not to copy that...I'm always working on something new...(it's) one of the prime reasons why I make music."

Prince recorded the bulk of *'Around the World in a Day'* between September and December, 1984, with the album's first batch of songs recorded at his usual studio at Sunset Sound in L.A., including *'Pop Life,' 'Temptation,' and 'Condition of the Heart,'* among others. In a signal of just how different a direction Prince was seeking to head in musically, in the few cases where he didn't play all of the instruments during sessions for the aforementioned songs, Prince introduced drummer Shelia E, with the drummer recalling the pair's first meeting back in 1979, that "I went backstage to tell him that I dug his music...I liked it because it was different and unpredictable, just like him. As soon as I went backstage, he came right up to me and said 'I know who you are.' I was shocked because he told me he was following my career. At the time, I was playing with George Duke but Prince wanted me to play drums for him. The first thing he asked me was how much I charged. I told him, and he said 'Well, I'll never be able to afford that.' We became friends then." In 1983, after Shelia sang a co-lead vocal on fan cult-favorite '*Erotic City*,' her first time behind a vocal mic, with the drummer recalling that "Prince asked me, 'Why don't you do your own album?' And I said 'Nah.'...I never wanted to sing until Prince asked me to. Lionel Richie had asked me to sing 'Endless Love,' on tour. I said 'You're crazy. I'm not going to do it.' You know, I get kind of scared when I hear my voice. When Prince asked me, though, I just had a feeling that he knew what he was talking about."

From '*Erotic City*,' the two expanded their musical collaboration to include the 1984 smash hit '*Glamouous Life*'—and album of the same title—with Shelia E, which went to #1 in 1984. Engineer Susan Rogers, who worked on the album, as well as later collaborations between Shelia E and Prince, explained at the time that Prince was instrumental in helping the drummer overcome her fear of the microphone because "Prince has a great ability to pull the best performances out of people...He can get performances out of people that didn't know they had it in them. And that was definitely the case with Shelia. He was able to get her to do things that she wouldn't have thought she could do." That foundation led to Prince's invitation in 1985 to Shelia to play drums on '*Pop Life*', which would become the biggest hit single off '*Around the World in a Day*.' While members of the Revolution were periodically around for recording sessions, Prince had also begun working with outside musicians on the album, notably including the aforementioned drummer, who, according to Susan Rogers, inspired Prince to abandon his beloved Lin drum machine for live drums on one of the album's tracks, '*Tamborine*,' recalling that "when he started to hang out with Shelia E and saw how she played drums, that fired him up."

When Prince was using live drums, Rogers recalled that "we used Yamaha (Hamamatsu, Japan) drums during the period of *Around the World in a Day*. The miking technique changed as a function of the song, the room, and the sound of the particular album. For programmed tracks, Prince primarily used the Linn LM-1 drum machine during the years I worked for him." Keyboardist Matt 'Dr.' Fink further offered that "Prince always had supplements to the Linns, like the Simmons drum brain, and the Sinsonic percussion unit, both of which were first implemented in 1999, but also used a lot on *Around the World in a Day*." Offering an example of how Prince's mood during the time-frame in which '*Around the World in a Day*' affected his performance in the studio, engineer Susan Rogers offered that "Prince played drums on '*Tamborine*' with such exuberance. He was gleeful that day and he loved that song, was in a great mood, and pounded the hell out of the drums." For Revolution drummer Bobby Z, the reality of Prince's universal musical talents—in terms of how it could affect the band's participation in recording sessions at any given moment, whether positively or negatively—was something his talent dictated those working around him simply accept as the norm, wherein, according to the drummer, "I've seen him write on everything. If you like '*Tambourine*' on *Around The World In A Day*, that's him writing on the drums...I think he's a great drummer. A very, very gifted keyboard player. But I think he's best on guitar. I think he's really a funky, solid bass player. I don't think there's a one-man band that just has the ability to play in various styles like he does." *Rolling Stone Magazine* seemed equally as impressed with his ability as Prince's band-mates, noting that in the course of making the album, "he holed up in the studio, as he usually does, to make *Around the World* virtually by himself. It's easy to forget, listening to the ping-pong of parts, that Prince puts his music together overdub by overdub—a triumph of planning as well as virtuoso execution. He lets friends in for background vocals and percussion and hires specialists for saxophone, cello, and oud (the North African lute), but all the essentials—guitars, synthesizers, drums, wolf whistles—are played by Prince alone."

Still, while Prince took full advantage of his one-man band abilities to capture the performances he wanted in the course of fleshing out '*Around the World in a Day*,' he also relied on the band for certain selections, with engineer Susan Rogers recalling that on another of that session's tracks, '*America*,' "each person stepped out and played...It must have been fun to play because they could just groove on that for hours. The band rehearsed it and we were ready to go. We put up a tape and pressed record. They played it and kept on playing until the tape ran out." Other songs which Prince featured the band in the recording of included "*Around the World in a Day*', which was recorded live with the band during rehearsal in Eden Prairie. He was recording day and night during that period and songs tended to get done very quickly. '*Nothing Compares 2 U,' 'America,' "Condition of the Heart,' 'God,'* and '*She's Always In My Hair'* were recorded then. We would sometimes start them at the warehouse and finish them in his home studio." Elaborating further on his recording process during this period, Prince conceded that "it is true I record very fast. It goes even quicker now that the girls help me—the girls, meaning Wendy and Lisa. I don't really think I left my funk roots anywhere along the line. *Around The World In A Day* is a funky album. Live it's even funkier."

In its review of the album, *Rolling Stone Magazine* would also make note of the fact that on *Around the World in A Day* Prince had "also reformulated the music. Now that everyone else is making funk tracks out of staccato keyboards, Prince has started to use sustained sounds: flutelike synthesizer." Of the multi-layers of synthesizers that Prince utilized in the course of the album's recording, keyboardist Matt 'Dr.' Fink recalled that "the Mirage samplers and the Yamaha DX 7's were extensively on *Around the World in a Day*. The flute sounds utilized on that song specifically were all DX7 flutes. He added the delay in the studio. There weren't any synthesizers that had on-board effects in those days, you had to have outboard pieces running on them, so we would use standard boss pedals for those effects. It was such a heavily-layered studio album that it was pretty hard to re-create live. On that album, we also had the Oberheim OBX-A and Omni synthesizers, as well another Oberheim that was more of a pre-set machine being utilized as well, which was a stripped down version of the X's, and had pre-sets on board you couldn't program. It was the kind of machine that just had banks of already-programmed stuff from the factory that were all the classic Oberheim sounds for less money, and was brought in for a supplement to the OBX's for fattener because there were a lot of usable sounds." For vocal tracks, engineer Susan Rogers added that Prince's preferred vocal mics were "either a Neumann U47 or an early version of the Sennheiser MD431."

Offering further detail to her background leading up to becoming Prince's primary recording engineer during what would become his most experimental musical period between 1985 and 1988, began by recalling that "in 1983, I heard that Prince was looking for an audio technician to maintain his home studio and I immediately contacted his management for an interview. Prince was my favorite artist ever since the 'For You' album and the opportunity was a dream come true. His management hired me and in August, 1983, I moved to Minnesota and got started by installing a new console in his home studio (his purple house on Kiowa Trail), and did some repairs on his tape machine. Next thing I knew, I was in the engineering chair...I loved music, but I wasn't a musician...I just always wanted to make records. I heard if you became an audio maintenance engineer, you'd always have a job...Prince needed an all-around engineer, one who could repair and use his equipment. I had to learn very quickly what sounds he liked but I was helped by a member of The Time, Jesse Johnson, who taught me how Prince liked the kick drum to sound, what reverb he liked on his vocal, what mics he used, etc. By the time Prince came home from the *Purple Rain* tour, I knew enough to be of great use to him in the studio... I was not a producer at that time. Prince produced and engineered his own albums, and I assisted him by setting everything up and keeping the equipment working. I would prepare the session by having the console and tape machine and his musical instruments ready to go, so all he had to do was sit down and record. I set the reverbs and outboard gear to the settings he preferred and recorded his band members when he asked me to."

Elaborating further, Rogers explained that her day-to-day routines with Prince—as with his past recording sessions—"were 24 hours long...You slept a few hours and started a new one...Prince worked very quickly and quietly. He liked to keep distractions to a minimum. If band members were overdubbing, he produced their tracks. He didn't do multiple takes; he preferred for us to punch in and fix mistakes as they happened. Sometimes band members and I would work alone to add parts while Prince was away. If band members or friends were around, Prince wouldn't take time away from a session to socialize." Other songs from the album recorded with Rogers at his new warehouse in Eden Prarie included '*Tambourine*,' '*America*,' and the records' biggest hit,

'*Raspberry Beret*,' with the engineer recalling that—in the case of the album's biggest hit single, it was "recorded live with the band during rehearsal in Eden Prairie. At the top of the track, Prince asks, 'Ready?' He was asking if I was in record mode. Lisa Coleman was asked to write the string arrangement. Lisa recruited string players from Los Angeles, including her brother David, to come to Minnesota. We recorded the strings as an overdub in the warehouse, using no isolation between the control room and recording space. This was in the days before Paisley Park, when Prince's home studio was too small to accommodate a lot of musicians at once… The console used for *Around the World in a Day* and *Sign O' The Times* was an API (Automated Processes, Inc., Jessup, Maryland)." Offering further detail on Prince's practice for introducing new songs from the album to the band during recording sessions, Rogers explained that "for songs where the band was used to record the basic tracks, he usually had the lyrics and melody before working out parts with the Revolution. There was never any pre-production as it is typically defined —a rough audio sketch of what the finished product might sound like. Prince was remarkable in his ability to make the appropriate artistic decisions while a song was taking shape. I am not saying that he never second-guessed or revisited his process, because he did. He was like any great producer —critical, skeptical, and honest."

In fleshing out the album's 9 studio tracks, Prince—revealing insight into his songwriting process for the record's eclectic musical compositions and arrangements—began by explaining that "when you're in the creative process, the first thing you naturally think about is the 'bombs,' the great ones that you've done before. You want to fill in the slots on your album with the songs that will make everyone the happiest: fans, musicians, writers, and so on. I used to try to fill those gaps first whenever I was trying something new, or wait to challenge myself to do another great one…I strive for perfection, and sometimes I'm a little bull-headed in my ways. Hopefully, people understand that there's just a lot on my mind and I try to stay focused on one particular thing. And I try not to hurt nobody in the process. A movie is a little bit more complex, but to me it's just a larger version of an album. There are scenes and there are songs, and they all go together to make this painting, and…I'm the painter. Y'all is the paintees."

Elaborating more in-depthly, Prince shared that "the sounds in my music are chosen with a lot of love too, and always with the idea of which color goes with which other color...Sometimes I'll be walking around and I'll hear the melody as if it were the first color in the painting. If you believe in the first color and trust it, you can build your song from there. Music is like the universe: Just look at how the planets, the air, and the light fit together...I'll start a track like that piece by piece. I'll have a color or a line in mind, and I'll keep switching things around until I get what I'm hearing in my head. Then I'll try to bring to Earth the color that wants to be with that first color. It's like having a baby, knowing that this baby wants to be with you. You're giving birth to the song...For instance, one-key songs designed to put the participant in a trance are best filled up with sound provoked by the spirit more than, say, a structural melody that's best complemented by color. This to me is the root of funk: the choices one makes...(The instruments I choose) depends on the song, it depends on the color. They all sound differently. It's very strange, I try to stay original in my work and a lot of sounds have been used now, and I'm looking for new instruments and new sounds and new rhythms. I got a lot of surprises...I don't want to give them all away."

Those surprises, according to Revolution guitarist Wendy Melvoin, came from the artist's being "hungry...by now...for different influences to take him further," while keyboardist Lisa Coleman added that "with Prince, what we were really doing and what he was interested in was doing a whole mix of things and really incorporating different sounds...(*Around the world in a Day*) has, I think, a huge mixture of different kinds of music, you know." Revolution keyboardist Matt 'Dr.' Fink, for his part, felt that "to me, that's his '*Sgt. Pepper*' because it was so experimental in nature and heavily layered." Still, Prince was quick to correct the impression that the album's psychedelic leanings had anything at all to do with the Beatles, explaining at the time that "What they say is that the Beatles are the influence. The influence wasn't the Beatles. They were great for what they did, but I don't know how that would hang today. The cover art came about because I thought people were tired of looking at *me*. Who wants another picture of him? I would only want so many pictures of my woman, then I would want the real thing. What would be a little more happening than just another picture would be if there was some way I could materialize in people's cribs when they play the record…I don't mind that (the record is called psychedelic), because that was the only period in recent history that delivered songs and colors."

Arguably the album's most literal composition—in terms of its lyrical attempt to spell out Prince's musical philosophy during his transition out of the Purple Rain era and into his next musical stratosphere—was *Paisley Park*, which he explained at the time "I've heard some people say that I'm not talking about anything on this record. And what a lot of other people get wrong about the record is that I'm *not* trying to be this great visionary wizard. *Paisley Park* is in everybody's heart. It's not just something that I have the keys to. I was trying to say something about looking inside oneself to find perfection. Perfection is in everyone. Nobody's perfect, but they can be. We may never reach that, but it's better to strive than not… I sorta had an f-you attitude, meaning that I was making something for myself and my fans. And the people who supported me through the years—I wanted to give them something and it was like my mental letter. And those people are the ones who wrote me back, telling me that they felt what I was feeling. Record sales and things like that…it really doesn't matter, ya know. It keeps a roof over your head, and keeps money in all these folks' pockets that I got hangin' around here! It basically stems from the music, and I'm just hoping that people understand that money is one thing but soul is another. That's all we're really trying to do, you know? I don't know. I wouldn't mind if I just went broke, you know, 'cuz as long as I can play this type of thing and come here, ya know. There were a lot of people there tonight and they turned the lights on and I looked up…it brings tears to your eyes because it's just—you can feel the love in the room, ya know? And that means more than money. I could just go on for hours…I don't know, I just have fun, and I'm thankful to be alive." Offering further insight into the latter, engineer Susan Rogers explained for Prince *Paisley Park* "summed up his philosophy. It was going to be his new statement, in other words, 'no longer Purple, we've got a new look, a new vision.' He was getting away from the purple and glitter, and into something new." Another aspect of that new musical direction involved Prince's decision to include his father in the album's writing, with Prince offering that

"He co-wrote '*The Ladder*' and several tunes on the new album. He's full of ideas. It'd be wonderful to put out an album on him, but he's a little bit crazier than I am." Engineer Susan Rogers further recalled that "this was a time when he was beginning to bring his father into his life, so his dad was around a lot. They were trying to develop a relationship. Prince gave his father songwriting credit (on the album)…It was a way to help him financially."

Released on April 22nd, 1985 with no advance press, the album debuted atop Billboard's Top 200 Album Chart at # 1, and produced 3 top 20 singles, including 'Raspberry Beret' (# 2), 'Pop life,' (# 7), and 'Paisley Park' (# 18). Prince, for his part, felt "the smartest thing I ever did was record *Around the World in a Day* right after I finished *Purple Rain*. I didn't wait to see what would happen with Purple Rain. That's why the two albums sound completely different. People think, 'Oh, the new album isn't half as powerful as *Purple Rain* or *1999*.'… I didn't want to make an album like the earlier ones…You know how easy it would have been to open *Around the World in a Day* with the guitar solo that's on the end of '*Let's Go Crazy*?' You know how easy it would have been to just put it in a different key? That would have shut everybody up who said an album wasn't half as powerful. I don't *want* to make an album like the earlier ones. Wouldn't it be cool to be able to put your albums back to back and not get bored, you dig?"

Critics did, including *Billboard Magazine*, who hailed the record for exactly what Prince seemed to be hoping they would, praising the records' "detailed production and intoxicating performances," while the *New York Times* hailed the album as Prince's "finest hour,' and the Washington Post declared the album as "one of the most intriguing albums in years." Regardless of what his critics felt, Prince seemed to feel the album was a hit in his own musical heart, as well as that of his fans and peers, sharing an example of the latter with one reporter at the time by explaining that "not long ago I talked to George Clinton, a man who knows and has done so much for funk. George told me how much he liked *Around the World in a Day*. You know how much more his words meant than those from some mamma-jamma wearing glasses and an alligator shirt behind a typewriter?" Looking back in hindsight on behalf of the Revolution, keyboardist Lisa Coleman recalled that "coming off such a huge success, it was an incredible album to make…We were all really cocky, but to come out with *'Around the World in a Day,'* which was experimental if self-indulgent, meant we still had enough sensibility…to try and grow musically, to make a statement." Prince, for his part, called the album "his favorite," and engineer Susan Rogers shared from her own observations that "he had confidence in making *Around the World in a Day…*He was at the happiest time in his life! He had a strong and clear vision." That vision would soon thereafter include a new film and motion picture soundtrack, as well as plans for his very own $10 million recording facility, not surprisingly entitled *'Paisley Park.'*

"Almost every sound on the record, vocal and instrumental, with the occasional exception of light percussion, saxophone, backing vocals and understated string arrangements, was made by Prince, who proves with this record that he has mastered the pop-rock idiom in the widest sense, from artsy rock to heavy metal, funk to sweet pop balladry."

—*New York Times*

Chapter 15:

'Parade: Music from the Motion Picture *Under the Cherry Moon'*—1986

If the title of Prince's next album was in any way indicative of the upbeat, inspired mood in the studio between him and his primary musical collaborators—Lisa Coleman and Wendy Melvoin—according to the latter member of the Revolution, "recording '*Parade*' was the best period for me...*Around the World in a Day* was a very private experience—it was a lot more isolated. Everything about *Parade* worked out so well—it was a great blend of funky, songy, without being psychedelic; it didn't fit into a genre. To me that album spoke individually to Prince's musical abilities.

It didn't sound like anybody else—it was just Prince doing something different. Musically, it reflected him the best." The album was recorded between June and July of 1985 primarily at Sunset Sound with Prince once again operating largely as a one-man band, as the Detroit Free Press would later note in its stellar review of the soundtrack album, noting that "the bulk of 'Parade' is listenable and enjoyable, a confirmation of Prince's place as a superior melodist, arranger and player as well as a celebration of his creativity," while the *New York Times* seemed once again dazzled by the fact that "almost every sound on the record, vocal and instrumental, with the occasional exception of light percussion, saxophone, backing vocals and understated string arrangements, was made by Prince, who proves with this record that he has mastered the pop-rock idiom in the widest sense, from artsy rock to heavy metal, funk to sweet pop balladry."

Offering fans a first-hand eye-witnessing of Prince's in-studio song construction in action, Revolution keyboardist Lisa Coleman recalled that—during the making of Parade—"the way he'd cut a song. You know, he'd start with the drums but he'd already have the song in his head... And he'd like go and press 'Record' on the machine and then run over to the drums and you'd kinda hear like him jumpin' over things and trippin' over wires, sit down on the drums, and then count himself off, tick, tick, tick. And then he'd like play and he'd like have, sometimes he'd have like—lyrics written down on a piece of notebook paper and so he'd try to like sing it in his head and sometimes you'd hear him like kinda grunting and singing a little bit of the song on the drum track. And then he'd imagine in his head like: he told me this, like you have to kick the bass player's ass. Like when you're playing the drums, like kick the other guy's ass, like put things in there that's gonna make the other guy—which was all him, you know, do something unexpected or like, try to keep up, you know. So it was so cool 'cause then he'd go do the drum track would be down and then he'd go and get the bass and play the bass and then that weird drum lick would come up and then he'd go, 'Oh,' you know, like the bass player, and then try to keep and then try to kick the guitar player's ass, etcetera, etcetera. And it was just really cool to sit there. Like, when I first moved out there, I stayed in his house for a while and we'd just be in the studio all the time, and sometimes I'd be the one punching 'em in or whatever. That was a lot of good stuff."

By far Prince's most eclectic blend of recorded instruments to date—drummer Bobby Z, in further describing Prince's creative process in bloom during this period, revealed that the variety of instruments Prince infused into the album's sound was a source of inspiration for him, such that "I've seen him write on everything… If you like keyboards, *'Under The Cherry Moon'* is that. If you like guitar, that's just about everything else…Another thing is that a new instrument will inspire him. A new keyboard instrument or a new kind of guitar, like in *'Girls And Boys,'* that synth guitar that whines like a duck. That inspired him to do that. Instruments could be inspiring for him, and I think being in the studio and new boards and new gear just keeps in fresh for him."

In terms of his writing process for the heavy presence of wind-instruments on the record, saxophonist Eric Leeds offered an inside look into this aspect of Prince's creative process by explaining that "he does not read or write music. At the time I was in the band, myself and the trumpeter Matt Blistan were the only guys that read music. Basically, everybody else would play by ear. But Prince knows the difference between say, an E minor chord and an E major, but as far as reading musical notation, he doesn't know how to do that. So basically, it would sometimes be a matter of him humming parts to me if there was a specific riff or lick. Or a lot of times he would look to me and say 'is there anything you hear on this?' Or if it was a solo he'd just open it up to me. You never knew specifically what the process would be on any given song until you started working on it. There were many times when he'd just leave a track in the studio with instructions for me to do something, but a lot of the times he'd give me a bunch of tracks and say 'go in and do anything you hear on it.' More often and not, he would not end up using a lot of the things I would do, but occasionally he might. The way I looked at it, is that if he ended up using something that I had contributed, fine. But if he didn't, the worst of it was that it gave me an opportunity to just work in the studio. You could not allow yourself to take any of this personally, whether he liked something or didn't like something, or the manner in which he liked something. Occasionally, I might have put an arrangement down on a song of his and he might have butchered it in my opinion. And I might think 'you've just destroyed the continuity of what I wanted to do,' but in the final analysis, what I was trying to do wasn't important. It's what he's hearing, because it's his music; it's his vision." Compositionally, Prince explained that, for *Parade*, "everything is sort of patterned after the 1st violet piano I received as a gift…Chords are important. Every note in a chord is a singer to me. This approach gives music its life. To look at music this way is a reason for living, as far as I'm concerned."

Still, while Prince was very much at the helm as usual during the making of Parade, it was his most conceptually collaborative in-studio experience to date, primarily via his collaborations with Wendy & Lisa—who co-wrote '*Mountains*' and '*Sometimes it Snows in April*', and Shelia E, all three of whom shared vocal duties in one form or another on a majority of the album's tracks, with keyboardist Matt 'Dr.' Fink recalling that "again, this was another album like '*Around the World in a Day*' where he did the majority of it, and had a lot of Lisa and Wendy on it, but the band wasn't very involved with that one. It was more Wendy and Lisa than anyone else. Mountains, for instance, I know began one of Lisa's compositions musically, and he sort of latched onto it—kind of like what he'd done with '*Dirty Mind*'—and turned it into a Prince song. They're both great writers and producers in their own right, and while I personally would have liked to have had more input, I was involved with other things, and Wendy and Lisa were around." Leeds further confirmed that "Wendy and Lisa and Sheila were around. This was a time when we were just going into the studio and jamming a lot…He had that relationship with other people, Sheila E particularly and of course Wendy and Lisa. From a conceptual basis, Wendy and Lisa were the two musicians in any of his bands who were able to tap into him on some subliminal level—they really did have a musical relationship that was closer than with anyone that he worked with…There were other times where he might have a starting point on a song and then midway through a line he might have said 'here's something, what do you hear off of that?' I might bounce something off of what he gave and he might bounce something off of me. And at the end of the song, I might be hard pressed to say what was mine and what was his—it really was a case of the whole being greater than the sum of the parts. Those were the circumstances that were more intriguing to me, because it was a matter of us trying to get into each other's heads...My relationship was a little bit more from a player's standpoint. Because of the tremendous drummer and percussionist that Sheila is, (it meant) that relationship was very important. Some of the more interesting and more enjoyable music from my point of view was when Sheila, Prince, Wendy and Lisa and I would just go into the studio and just jam. I've got quite a few tapes of sessions like that. Purely ad lib, instrumental sessions, where we'd go in and just make a lot of music. None of it was going to get released; it was for our own enjoyment. Wendy and Lisa don't really come from a jazz background [but] they shared in the ability to be very spontaneous. Our ability to go in and spontaneously play some music and at the end of an hour come out with some music that at least we could say has some kind of musical validity and continuity. It may not have the harmonic sophistication of a straight-up jazz band, but the ethic was very similar. When Prince wanted to be spontaneous, he could be very spontaneous!...We were doing a lot of spontaneous stuff, particularly with Shelia E. That's the closest we got to the jazz concept."

Offering a greater depth of insight into why Prince felt such a creative connection to Wendy and Lisa during this period, Revolution keyboardist Lisa Coleman revealed that "the three of us started quite a love affair...We travelled together, we'd spend a lot of time together in Nice while he was shooting *Under The Cherry Moon*. He trusted us...The three of us really had a special relationship and it's unbreakable...I really love him. He's like a brother to me. We did things that only happen in your dreams, they were some of the best times of my life. He's such a talented person, so creative." Keyboardist Matt 'Dr.' Fink, for his own part, observed during this period that Prince was "totally favoring Wendy and Lisa...He started vibing off of them, their writing, production work, and everything else." Camped out with Prince in Studio 3 at Sunset Sound Studios, where Leeds recalled that "we spent a lot of time in L.A., where we were doing the bulk of our recording," the studio had become a second home to Prince by this point in the mid-1980s, such that, as studio manager Craig Hubler recalled that "everybody at Sunset Sound was so familiar with him now that he felt like part of a family. He felt secure and comfortable coming here. He was used to having a bed in the studio, just kind of lay there on his stomach with his notepad in front of him to write his lyrics. So we arranged to have a queen-sized bed in the studio, which we set up in the performance area in the middle of the room. I brought purple sheets and a purple bedspread." Still, Prince hardly slept, and within the first day of recording, on April 17th, 1985, he laid the basic instrumental tracks to *'Wendy's Parade,' 'New Position,' 'I Wonder You,'* and *'Under the Cherry Moon,'* with engineer Susan Rogers recalling a pace wherein "after we had everything set up…he wanted me to make sure we were ready because once he got started he didn't want to stop. He said 'I'm gonna start playing drums, and when I stop, don't stop the tape. Just keep going, let it roll.' He sat down behind the drum set and taped his lyrics up on a music stand in front of him. We pressed record on the tape machine and he played the entire drum track to four songs in a row. Four drum tracks, just in a row, all first takes. We never cut in between those songs. They were made as they were… Then he came back in and said 'Alright, here we go! Where is my bass?' And he began overdubbing on all four songs. It was clear that this was going to be the start of the record in a big way."

Of the album's highly-experimental sound, Rogers explained that during this period, "he liked having more tools around him in the studio to work with. Previously he just wanted to have one or two reverbs and stick with those. Now he had a lot of money and he wasn't afraid to rent a new piece of gear just to try out for a week or so, and if he liked it, he'd end up buying it. When he would approach a piece of gear like that, he certainly would not bother to read the manual. He'd just go through it and find programs that sounded cool, then he'd either overdrive it or just crank up the returns till things were really wet." Of the production on the album's rhythm tracks, Rogers recalled that Prince "was becoming a much better drummer…Working with Shelia influenced him a lot… He felt a lot more confident and became a pretty good drummer. He still liked using the LM-1, but he wanted some other options." As for keyboards utilized during the album's tracking, Revolution keyboardist Matt 'Dr.' Fink recalled that, in addition to the Fairlight, "the DX-7 was used on Parade, the Omnis and Oberheims were still around as usual, but I also remember we added on a Kurzweil *Music Systems K250* keyboard, which was the very first sample-playing keyboard. It was useful because it had really good string samples on it, orchestral sounds, which we used on both *Around the World in a Day* and *Parade*, where Clare wasn't doing the string parts."

When attention turned to the album's biggest hit, '*Kiss*,' which *Rolling Stone Magazine* praised by pointing out that "rhythmically, '*Kiss*' is funk; harmonically, it is rhythm & blues; lyrically, it proves Prince is crossing yet another frontier, into emotional maturity," fellow engineer David Rivkin recalled a truly inspired studio session in which—CONTRARY to BASELESS rumors that another band Mazarati had originally written the song and Prince thereafter had bought the band out of its rights to the hit—Prince had written the song's original demo on an acoustic guitar at Sunset Sound, whereafter "we didn't know what to do with the song...It was just an acoustic guitar version." Prince, for his own part in commenting on his inspiration for the song, explained that "you go to a higher plane (of creativity) with that. They don't sound like anything else. '*Kiss*' doesn't sound like anything else. They aren't conscious efforts; you just have to get them out. They're gifts. Terence Trent D'arby asked me where '*Kiss*' came from, and I have no idea. Nothing in it makes sense. Nothing! The high-hat doesn't make sense." Once in the studio to work on the song, Rivkin continued, recalling that he and Prince "turned it into a groove. We came up with this drum beat and gated the acoustic guitar to the hi-hat of the drum machine. The guitar is playing the same rhythm that the hi-hat is doing, but it's playing the changes the acoustic guitar did. We added bass," with Prince chiming in on the addition of the song's unique bass line, that "(as with) '*When Doves Cry*', the bass is in the kick drum. It's the same with '*Kiss*': The bass is in the tone of the reverb on the kick. Bass is a lot more than that instrument over there. Bass to me means B-A-S-E." Offering additional commentary on the song's production, Revolution keyboardist Matt 'Dr.' Fink recalled that "it was a Linn drum machine pulsing through the loop, and then the main guitar rhythm is actually an acoustic guitar that Prince is actually strumming on the one of each chord of each bar, so every time the hi-hat is hit, it opened up a gate which opened up the guitar and made it sound like it was pulsing along the hi-hat track. It's called 'Side chain gating.' Then that synth-marimba vibe that comes in was played on a DX-7 synthesizer."

Once principle recording on the album's twelve tracks was completed, Prince handed the record over to legendary orchestral composer/arranger Clare Fisher for his own creative additions, the first in what would be a long-standing relationship of implicit creative trust to blossom thereafter between Prince and Clare throughout the remainder of the 1980s and into the early 1990s. Of their first collaboration together in the course of making 'Parade,' engineer Susan Rogers began by explaining that "Clare's work involved a lot of counter-melody and movement...(It was) a Prince album with input by Clare." Fisher, for his part, revealed in discussing his long-standing relationship with Prince that "we haven't met personally.... My relationship with Prince is that he heard of my writing through Rufus and Chaka Khan and although I was not basically what you would call a rock musician, here again my classical training came to the front My favorite instrumentation as a writer is that of the symphony orchestra, although I have written for many different types of things, my preference lies here...(I work mostly on) the structure of the song, because that's what I fit my arrangement to... I think the reason that I got writing for pop artists in the first place is the fact that they felt I added a layer of sophistication to their music."

In a demonstration of just how eager Prince was to expand the musical pallet of his sound, Fisher shared of their collaboration that "first of all he has left me completely free. It is a wise man who after he hires someone, does not interfere with his product. Prince was very open in this area. I think besides being a jazz writer, I have written for classical instrumentations, and that's how unlike most jazz writers, who have a non-classical concept of tone, I was orchestrally well versed... One of the good features at the beginning especially was that he allowed me freedom and space to make value judgments...(With) the fact that he allows me complete freedom in what I do....one would think that he would have a tremendous ego which would interfere with your relationship. Prince does have a strong ego but he is not the kind who tries to superimpose that on you."

Elaborating on the inner-workings of their collaborative process, Fisher explained that "he sends me a cassette tape of his recording, and then I have my son, Brent, transcribe it. Then I write my arrangement in conjunction with this transcription... I have a great joy in writing for strings and one of the problems with this in the recording studio is money to pay musicians, so people are given such low budgets that you can't hire a large string section. Prince spends money and so I was able to write string sections as opposed to writing for a small string ensemble." Amazingly, from their first collaboration forward thereafter, Fisher revealed that "I've never met Prince, and I was informed by people who had been with him that when asked about meeting me, he said, 'I don't want to meet him. It's going just fine as it is.'...Most people want to tell you exactly what they want for an arrangement but then again they are not the writers so there is always a superimposition of their limited scope on what they conceive. A writer has to fight to get what he does. The worst person in conjunction with this is the producer who thinks that he has a special orientation toward what it should be. That's like comparing apples and bananas. I think that I was accepted by Prince because of that fact. . . the fact that my writing was of a professional level through years of experience."

Released on March 31st, 1986, 'Parade: Music from the Motion Picture *Under the Cherry Moon*' debuted at # 3 on Billboard's Top 10 Album Chart, selling 4 million copies worldwide, and spawning three hit singles with the SMASH '*Kiss*' (# 1 US), '*Girls & Boys*' (#11 on the UK chart), and '*AnotherLoverHoleinYourHead*' (# 18 R&B), and '*Mountains*' (# 23 US). In spite of the fact that the film itself was a MAJOR flop, the album was a critic darling, beginning with *Rolling Stone Magazine*'s declaration that "most of '*Around the World in a Day*' like an exercise in pop psychedelia instead of a full-fledged immersion in it. Luckily, *Parade*...fitted a leaner, more finely polished psychedelia with a healthy shot of funk... This is the degree of energy and intelligence we have come to expect from Prince. This is the promise he has once again kept—on *Parade*. Like *Purple Rain*, the new album is a soundtrack (for the forthcoming *Under the Cherry Moon*) and is preceded by the stunning *Kiss.*"

Continuing, the magazine notes that while "few of us are visionaries… in the arrangements on *Parade*, it is Prince's vision to that is paraded: a simple Weillen waltz like *'Under the Cherry Moon'* proves an excuse for all manner of orchestral invention; when Prince says on *'New Position,'* 'You've got to try my new funk,' believe him. In *'New Position,'* on *'Kiss'* and above all in the sensational *'Girls & Boys,'* Prince conceives a clean, diamond-hard style that could spawn years of imitations…Far from the funk of *Dirty Mind*, this style springs from an understanding of orchestration, rather than the innate ability to jam on rhythm instruments. On *Parade*, all sounds—snippets of guitar, horn, percussion, voice—are treated equally, erasing the line between 'basic track' and 'sweetening.' Prince has achieved the effect of a full groove using only the elements essential to a listener's understanding—and so has devised a funk completed only by the listener's response." The Detroit Free Press, for its part, complimented Prince's progress in retaining "the psuedo-psychedelic edge—and makes better use of it—than he did on last year's album, *Around the World in a Day*…The gems on *'Parade'* are unquestionably the foot-movers…But Prince is equally effective when he about-faces on *'Venus De Milo,'* a soft piano-saxophone duet, and *'Sometimes It Snows in April.'* " Melody Maker, for its part, declared that "*Parade* eclipses everything else you've heard this year!"

Upon release to the public, it was clear one musical era was coming to an end and another beginning with the release of *'Parade,'* with longtime Revolution drummer Bobby Z recalling that, by that point, "I think that the band became cold, but I don't think the *Parade* tour was cold. I think that when the band was unshackled from giant arenas with giant soundstages, and having to do 'rigid' shows, it was still a pretty funky band. I don't think that it was that good at improvisational music." Clearly more of the direction Prince was musically desiring to head in by that point in his almost 10 year career, with the artist for his own part explaining that "I felt we all needed to grow, we all needed to play a wide range of music with different types of people…No band can do everything." Engineer Susan Rogers, who would continue working with Prince over the course of *'Sign O'the Times'* and *'The Black Album'*, for her part, added that, from her recollections at the time of the Revolution's disbandment, "he wanted to evolve from his previous sound and was eager to expand his sound as well as his songwriting…He wanted it to sound a little bigger and more polished and fully produced than his records had in the past." Saxophonist Eric Leeds, from a musical vantage point, further offered that "the time leading up to the release of *Parade* was a time when Prince was interested in seeing where he could go artistically…He was growing as a composer, getting involved with Miles Davis." Leeds would stay on as saxophonist part of Prince's new post-Revolution touring band, along with Shelia E, who replaced drummer Bobby Z, and Levi Ceasar Jr., who replaced Marc Brown on bass, as well as sole Revolution holdover Matt 'Dr.' Fink on keyboards, although the Revolution stayed together for a brief tour in support of *Parade*. Of Shelia E's decision post-working with Prince in the studio on 'Parade' to join his band, she explained that—in spite of her success as a solo artist thanks to the Prince-written/produced '*Glamorous Life*'—"I wanted to get away from the pressure of being a solo artist. It was important for me to get back to playing the drums because I was just tired of having a band and being the one out front all the time."

Paisley Park Studios

7801 Audubon Road, Chanhassan, MN

The Atrium

Studio A

NEVER BEFORE SEEN photos of Paisley Park's studio B where Prince worked out of, with his instruments set up, his drum set, his vocal mic (he sang at the console), etc.

AND MOST VALUABLY...HIS VAULT!!

During this same time, amid the release and promotion of '*Parade*,' engineer Susan Rogers recalled that "a lot of material was being written and recorded and Prince's new studio, Paisley Park, was in the early stages of planning...I also helped the design team of Paisley Park Studios and made decisions on the purchase of new recording gear." Built with $10 million in financing from Warner Bros. as part of his contract re-negotiation, Prince fulfilled a life-long dream with the construction of Paisley Park Studios in Chanhassen, Minnesota. Just a mile's drive from his newly-completed 3,000 square-foot Mansion, built on a 30-acre property he'd bought in 1985, engineer Susan Rogers recalled that the house "was nice for him...(because he could) incorporate his social life into his home...He had what he'd always wanted: people around him. They would go upstairs and watch TV or sit in the kitchen for hours telling jokes." The house of course boasted a state-of-the-art home studio, which Prince often trafficked back and forth between trips home from Paisley Park Studios, which was very much under construction in 1986. Philosophically, Prince explained at the time that "Paisley Park is an alternative. I'm not saying it's greater or better. It's just something else. It's multicolored, and it's very fun...Paisley Park is the place one should find in oneself, where one can go when one is alone...I basically come in the back entrance and just pretty much use the studios."

"The wide range of Prince's musicianship comes through much more clearly here than it did in 'Purple Rain'!"

—*Rolling Stone Magazine,*
Review of 'Sign O'the Times'

Chapter 16:

Sign O'the Times—1987

Though opinions among fans will invariably contrast, most critics universally consider *'Sign O'the Times'* Prince's unsurpassed studio masterpiece, with *Rolling Stone Magazine* hailing it as "Prince's pinnacle," while the *New York Times* was enchanted enough to observe that "Prince, whose ties to soul and jazz are clearer than ever before, whose willingness to embrace different musical forms seems to grow all the time, has never cast a stronger spell." *Time Magazine* even felt compelled to "give the man credit" in its review of the double LP, making it clear that Prince's decision to disband the Revolution in favor of returning to his one-man-band roots hadn't been in commercial vain. *Billboard Magazine,* for its part, observed that on the 18-song opus, Prince "sounds liberated, diving into territory merely suggested on *Around the World in a Day* and *Parade*...The music overflows with generous spirit." Explaining his musical rationale behind the 18-song opus, Prince reasoned that "what people were saying about *'Sign O'the Times'* was 'there are some great songs on it,' and 'there are some great experiments on it'…I hate the word 'experiment.' It sounds like something you didn't finish. Well, they have to understand that's the way to have a double album and make it interesting."

Prince began work on '*Sign O'the Times*' in March of 1986 in his newly finished state-of-the-art home recording studio, which in-house engineer Susan Rogers recalled was "a world-class studio…We really could have competed with anything. Unlike the previous house, it actually had a small, isolated studio part where you could set up drums and piano. The control room was a beautiful room…(with) stained glass windows." Describing the record-a-holic work routine she had settled into with Prince as his primary in-house engineer over the course of her work on '*Around the World in a Day*' and '*Parade: Music from the Motion Picture Under the Cherry Moon*', Susan Rogers recalled that "a typical day for me began in the early afternoon. As far as I know Prince used the morning to attend to the business of running his company. Once we started we would work all through the night and finish in the early morning of the next day. We would often record for more than 24 consecutive hours."

In attempting to explain what drove his amazing work ethic, Prince reiterated, as he had in the past, that it was largely out of his hands because his "music is made out of necessity…You're not even its maker, you're just there to bring it forth…I make music because if I didn't, I'd die. I record because it's in my blood…The only time I feel like a prisoner…is when I think too much and can't sleep from just having so many things on my mind. You know, stuff like, 'I could do this, I could do that., I could work with this band. When am I going to do this show or that show?' There's so many things. There's women. Do I have to eat? I wish I didn't have to eat…I work a lot, and there's not too much time for anything else when I'm doing that…You see, I get these ideas, sometimes at 4 a.m…So I get up, get dressed and come and sit (in the studio) until it's over…That's the thing: I have to finish a song to clear my mind for the next idea." As the only hold-out from the recently-disbanded Revolution, keyboard player Matt Fink recalled, the effects of the latter were "difficult to deal with…When Prince is pretty much playing everything…you're left out of the creative process." Still, ultimately, as then-manager Alan Leeds pointed out, for Prince it was never personal, simply because the artist "seldom behaved as if recording was a job...It was simply what he did—day in, day out."

In order to allow for as much time as possible in the studio to get one musical idea out of his head before the next arrived and took its place as he crafted '*Sign O'the Times*,' Prince maintained an all-business atmosphere in the studio, wherein in-house engineer Susan Rogers explained that "he allowed people to stay in the control room for a session as long as they were quiet and didn't interrupt him. Frequently it was just the two of us during those years...He liked working with people who were quiet and who had a lot of endurance." For his own part, Prince reasoned that, in order to properly channel his frequent floods of creativity during recording sessions, "I use engineers in shifts a lot of the time because when I start something, I like to go all the way through...There will be times when I've been working in the studio for twenty hours and I'll be falling asleep in the chair, but I'll still be able to tell the engineer what cut I want to make...There are very few musicians who will stay awake that long."

Detailing her observations of Prince's songwriting routine during the recording of *Sign*, engineer Susan Rogers recalled that in large part, there wasn't one, such that "the probability of Prince coming to the studio with a melody and lyrics was, as I recall, equally as likely as his coming in with nothing written down. When he came in with lyrics he would sometimes tape them to a rack tom so that he could record drums while following the text. There would be many sessions where he would record the drums, bass, and chord progression on a keyboard, and then make a cassette and leave the studio to write lyrics." Whether writing in the studio or out, to keep pace with his hyper-driven recording schedule, Rogers recalled of Prince's technical set-up during the *Sign O' The Times* that "Prince recorded to 24-track analog. We did not synchronize to a second machine, primarily because it takes time (a few to several seconds) for two machines to locate to the same point in the material and lock their tape drives to the same clock. Every now and then the two machines would have difficulty locking and so the system would have to be rebooted. Prince preferred to limit his recording to only 24 tracks rather than wait for two machines to synchronize and give him 48 tracks."

Recorded between Prince's home studio in Minneapolis and out in L.A. at Sunset Sound, Prince's chief engineer Susan Rogers recalled that, whether in Minnesota or L.A., Prince placed an important emphasis on sonic consistency, recording on an "API Console similar to the console in Studio 3 at Sunset Sound, where he liked to work. Both consoles were customized by Frank Demidio for expanded dynamic and frequency range. Some material from *Sign of the Times* was recorded at band rehearsal using a Soundcraft (Herts, U.K.) console (I don't remember the model but it was similar to their discontinued 'Ghost')." Beginning as he always did with drums, Rogers recalled that "if the drums didn't sound great, he felt it was building a song on a weak foundation." For those songs on *Sign* in which Prince utilized programmed drums, Rogers cited his favorite as the Linn LM-1, such that he found it consistently "amazing, the different sounds he could get out of it." Citing one example of just how profoundly *Sign O'the Times'* broader musical direction—in the context of experimentation—was influenced by the Linn, engineer Susan Rogers cites '*Starfish and Coffee*', wherein Prince played backward after the rhythm track was laid, such that the experiment was "all part of the song being about opening your mind to other possibilities," clearly a theme in the course of the recording of the broader '*Sign O'the Times*' album.

For live drums, Rogers recalled that "we used Yamaha (Hamamatsu, Japan) drums." Delving into Prince's specific micing techniques, Rogers recalled that "when a close-miked technique was called for, we sometimes used an Electro-Voice (Bosch Communications Systems, Minneapolis, MN) RE20, AKG (AKG Acoustics GmbH, Vienna, Austria) D112, or the Sennheiser MD421 on the kick drum. The snare drum usually was miked with the SM57 on top and an AKG 451 on the bottom. Sennheiser MD441 and 421s were used for toms. An AKG 451 was used for the hi-hat. The overhead mics were chosen after considering the size of the room (we recorded in Prince's home studio, at rehearsal, at Sunset Sound, and on the road during that time). The Neumann U47s or U87s might be used as room mics, or a pair of AKG 414s. The small percussion (clave, claps, toms, etc.) was typically routed through one or a few Boss (Roland Corporation, Los Angeles, CA) effects pedals such as the Flanger, Chorus, Overdrive, Delay, Distortion, Tremolo, etc."

When turning from drums to a bass sound that *Rolling Stone Magazine* called "the star, so sweet it's giving up melodies, so expressive you know it's talking to you in another language, so funky that if you ain't groovin' you might be dead," engineer Susan Rogers recalled that Prince's bass "was typically recorded using the direct signal only, although Prince frequently would use effects pedals between the instrument and the direct box. Any microphones on the bass amp/cabinet were used primarily in live mixing, as I recall. Because recordings were limited to 24 tracks, it was not customary to separately record the clean, direct bass sound and the instrument's sound through an amp and cabinet." Following bass, Prince typically next turned his attention to what *Rolling Stone* again praised as "irresistible keyboard riff(s)," and the *New York Times* hailed as "keyboard-driven funk that he synthesized from James Brown, Sly and the Family Stone and disco is now dispensed by everyone from Ready for the World to Janet Jackson. Prince needs to stay ahead of his imitators; he's also looking over his shoulder at the Beatles and Sly Stone." Prince's chief sonic assistant Rogers detailed his favored synthesizers as including "the "Fairlight Computer Music Instrument (Fairlight, Sydney, Australia), the Yamaha DX-7, and the Oberheim (Gibson Musical Instruments, Nashville, TN) OB-Xa were the main keyboards in use at that time, along with piano…Prince played a Hammond (Addison, IL) B3 so I used a stereo pair of AKG 414s on the top rotor and often an MD421 or AKG D112 on the lower rotor of the Leslie cabinet."

Sign O'the Times marked Prince's return to guitar glory, with *Rolling Stone Magazine* pointing out that the artist's latest licks were moving him steadily "toward guitar-god status," while Rogers recalled that, from a technical angle, the "signal routing of the guitar was determined by the song. Most rhythm guitar tracks used a clean sound that took the direct signal through Boss effects pedals and an active direct box such as the Countryman (Countryman Associates, Inc., Menlo Park, CA) Type 85. Distorted electric guitar tracks were recorded by miking the Bag End (Bag End Loudspeakers, Lake Barrington, IL) guitar cabinets patched to a Mesa/Boogie (Mesa/Boogie, Petaluma, CA) amplifier head. Shure SM 57s and Sennheiser MD421s were the mikes of choice for guitar." When tracking his guitar overdubs for any of the album's 16 tracks, Rogers recalled that "Prince preferred to record in the control room so the signal from the guitar was routed to the amp using a pair of passive direct boxes to minimize signal loss."

When turning his attention to what most critics and fans alike consider to be among the most mature and electric vocal performances of Prince's career, engineer Susan Rogers detailed a recording routine wherein "We'd get the track halfway or three-quarters of the way there and then set him up with a microphone in the control room. He'd have certain tracks on the multi-track that he would use and he'd do the vocal completely alone. I think that was the only way he could really get the performance." In choosing a mainstay microphone for vocal performing, Rogers recalled Prince's typical preference as either a "Neumann U47 or a Sennheiser 441 dynamic microphone, recommended by Stevie Nicks." When Prince turned his ear to vocal effect layering, Rogers explained that their routine was to add "effects as we added tracks so that once the overdubs were finished, we could mix without much more work. Signal processors such as limiters and compressors and equalizers were recorded to tape. At the start of each session I would patch in the reverbs, delays, and other effects that he liked. As the session progressed and the song took shape, the effects would be modified to suit the arrangement." When recording wind instruments, which *Rolling Stone Magazine* pointed out came via "assists from two estimable horn men, sax player Eric Leeds and trumpeter Atlanta Bliss," Rogers recalled that she "used the Neumann U47, U87, and the AKG 414s most often for these instruments."

In identifying some of the broader effects Prince preferred to use in the studio during the album's recording, Rogers recalled that "we used the U.A. model 1176 and LA-3A limiters for guitars and piano. A Lexicon Prime Time Model 93 was used for delays and chorusing. While at Sunset Sound we used the live chambers and plates for most of the reverbs. At home in Minnesota we had a Publison Infernal Machine (Bagnolet, France), the Lexicon (Woodbury, NY) models PCM60, 200, and 480L, and an Electrical Measuring Technology (EMT-FRANZ GmbH,

Mahlberg, Germany) model 244 to use for reverb sounds. Prince's preferred vocal limiter was the LA 2A from Universal Audio (U.A. Scotts Valley, CA). An indispensable tool was the Eventide (Eventide, Inc., Little Ferry, N.J.) H910 for adding a chorusing effect to vocals or for converting a mono signal into a faux-stereo effect."

While album tracks like '*Hot Thing*' and '*Forever in My Life*' were recorded at Prince's home studio in August, 1986, in October, 1986, Prince returned with Susan Rogers to Sunset Sound in Los Angeles to continue work on what would become much of '*Sign O'the Times*' final track listing, where he stayed locked away for the better part of the remainder of 1986. Songs completed during these sessions include '*Play in the Sunshine,*' '*Adore*', and '*U Got the Look.*' Of the latter tune, which *Time Magazine* would single out as "born to be a dance hit," and would indeed become the album's first hit single, engineer Susan Rogers recalled that "this was recorded over Thanksgiving in Los Angeles at Sunset Sound. The recording was one of the longest productions during my time with Prince. It was originally a much slower track. He spent a long time building the arrangement, only to ultimately speed it up and erase a lot of what he had recorded (very unusual). While the faster track was taking shape, Sheena Easton came by the studio. I don't know if Prince planned to have her sing on the track and called her in (they had met recently) or if she just came by and he took advantage of the opportunity. She agreed to sing on it and I remember him asking her if she needed to warm up first. She said 'no' and he was impressed. The entire song took several days from start to finish —typical of 99.9% of the recording world but unusual for Prince." Addressing the making of another of the album's hit singles, '*I Could Never Take the Place of Your Man*', which *Rolling Stone Magazine* praised for "its Who-like crunch chords and its irresistible keyboard riff," Rogers explained that, for Prince, "revisiting a song from the vault was very rare during that period...'*I Could Never Take The Place Of Your Man*' was an older track pulled from the vault for *Sign O' the Times*. It featured a Linn (Roger Linn Design, Berkley, CA) LM-1 drum machine."

Delving into more exciting moments behind the recording of a collection of songs wherein, according to *Billboard Magazine*, "Prince shows nearly all of his cards here, from bare-bones electro-funk and smooth soul to pseudo-psychedelic pop and crunching hard rock, touching on gospel, blues, and folk along the way," engineer Susan Rogers begins with the album's title track, recalling that "*Sign O'the Times* was "recorded at Sunset Sound in one 10-hour session, with engineer Susan Rogers recalling afterward that "we all recognized how profound that song was...It was amazing: a great lyric and a great vocal, beautifully done. The sound of the song was due to the Fairlight. He was able to sit down at the Fairlight and get such a cool sound from it." Regarding 'The Ballad of Dorothy Parker,' which inspired *Rolling Stone Magazine* to point out that "Prince's virtuoso eclecticism has seldom been so abundantly displayed," engineer Susan Rogers explained of the song's quirky, compressed vocal effect that, during the vocal's recording, "I noticed there was something wrong: there was no high-end at all, half the new console wasn't working. It could have been remixed, but Prince loved it the way it was." Of Prince's inspiration for the song, Rogers recalled him explaining it had come from a dream about the literary legend, wherein he'd commented afterward on his inspiration that "I remember him talking about how wonderful that was when a song comes to you in a dream. You wake up and it's like somebody has given you a gift."

Turning to arguably the album's most provocative and controversial song, '*If I Was Your Girlfriend*,' which *Billboard Magazine* termed to be "the most disarming and bleak psycho-sexual song Prince ever wrote," engineer Susan Rogers focused from a recording standpoint on vocals that NME explained found Prince "adapting to his falsetto voice over an hypnotic, brooding groove, Prince switches genders to detail his romantic notions," with the engineer recalling that "the song was recorded at Sunset Sound, Studio 3. The microphone preamplifiers added gain in 10 dB steps, rather than in a continuous sweep. In the case of '*If I Was Your Girlfriend*,' the pre amp gain was accidentally set 10 dB too hot for the vocal channel. The result was a pretty nasty distortion, although he never complained about it. I did not notice until too late because Prince recorded his vocals alone in the control room. I would set up the vocal signal path with the mic and equalization and limiter, and then patch it to a track. After the headphone mix was ready, Prince worked alone until the vocals (lead and backing) were finished."

Continuing, Rogers explained that "the timbre of the vocal on '*If I Was Your Girlfriend*' was achieved using a trick that Prince often used for voice or guitar. The tape machine was slowed down for the recording, using a variable speed control. The speed was returned to normal for playback, resulting in a 'high-speed' sound. On guitar tracks, the machine might be brought down to half speed for the recording; but on vocals it was typically tuned to a lower key, although not as low as an octave…(So the vocal) was an accident on my part…I set him up with his mic and left the room, and I just inadvertently had something switched the wrong way that day and when I came back…into the control room and listened to…the finished vocal, I thought 'Oh No!' It was so distorted. I thought, 'He's going to kill me.' He never said a word…He liked the sound of it, I guess. He never said a word about it…He had this attitude, well, maybe that was meant to be. He was good about those things."

Turning to another of the album's songs which featured the same sped-up vocal technique utilized on '*If I Was Your Girlfriend*,' engineer Susan Rogers recalled that "during the recording of '*Housequake*,' we were at Sunset Sound in LA and recorded every day and night during that time period so I am sorry to say I don't have much in the way of specific memories of that song. I do remember that it was one of the songs he spent a long time on which usually meant (I assume) that the song was one he considered especially important or he particularly enjoyed working on. I remember that it came at a time when there were other changes in his life; his musical instruments, his style, his colors, and the people around him were evolving. It is only my guess but I think *Housequake* represented a new idea in dance music for him." Of '*The Cross*,' which the *Philadelphia Daily News* called "a soft, lovely gospel number," and *Buzz Magazine* pointed out "starts as a ballad and builds to one of the most satisfying rock arrangements he's ever done," Rogers recalled that the song "was recorded at Sunset Sound, Studio 3, and a sparse, open miking technique was used. It might have been a Sennheiser (Wennebostel, Germany) MD421 on the kick drum, a Shure (Chicago, IL.) SM57 on the snare, and a pair of Neumann (Berlin, Germany) U47 tube mics positioned as a stereo pair over the kit."

Released on March 31ˢᵗ, 1987, 'Sign O'the Times' produced Top 10 hits with its title track, 'U Got the Look,' and 'I Could Never Take the Place of Your Man,' (#'s 3, 2 and 10 on the Billboard Hot 100 Singles Chart), quickly selling 2 million copies. The double-LP marked a comeback of sorts for Prince with his critics, with the *New York Times* pointing out at the start of its 5-star review of the album that "in some ways, Prince has retrenched for 'Sign o'the Times.' It's harder-edged, less orchestral and more danceable than his last two albums...After his movie-video-record blockbuster, 'Purple Rain,' whose soundtrack sold more than 10 million copies...'Around the World in a Day' (which sold three million copies) and 'Parade' (1.8 million)...did comparatively poorly... Prince clearly hopes to regain the commercial momentum he sacrificed...yet he's not abandoning what he learned, he's consolidating it, extending his music while stripping away mumbo-jumbo." Clearly won over by the album's sheer span of unbridled brilliance, the NY Times went on to focus in praise on the fact that "virtually all by himself, Prince is a more versatile, more eclectic band than ever. Like the Beatles, he picks and chooses from everything that catches his ear, mixing allusions until they add up to something like originality." Another critical convert, *Entertainment Weekly*, meanwhile, reported that "back in form, Prince finally delivers the goods he'd been promising in the wake of Purple Rain. From topical funk...to unabashed pop...to glorious guitar squalor to simmering R&B, this double album was a sign that proved worth heeding."

Picking up on the NY Times' critical narrative concerning his unrivaled originality, *Rolling Stone Magazine* pleasantly quipped that "Prince is beginning to be a puzzlement. *Sign O'the Times*, his ninth album in what is now a nine-year recording career, is of course largely dazzling; sixteen tracks spread across two LPs—half of them brilliant, half merely better than ninety percent of the stuff you hear on the radio. There really is no one else like him (although a lot of people try to be), and he remains that rare pop artist to whom you can attach the word genius...Simple virtuosity—mere brilliance, one might almost say—seems too easy an exercise, at this point, for someone of Prince's extraordinary gifts." Still, no one was accusing Prince of being creatively idle, with *Blender Magazine* pointing to the fact that "stamina—the ability to funk until dawn—has always been Prince's strong suit. So while this double album runs the gamut from house to Hendrix, R&B ballads to shimmering power pop, its creator's energy never seems to flag...A masterpiece." NME Magazine concluded for its part that the album "once again pays testimony to the man's musical unpredictabilty and insatiable appetite for new styles and moods...(and) his talent for writing unsurpassable contemporary music," while *Buzz Magazine* hailed it as "the work of an unabashed, unsurpassed pop master."

Nominated for a Grammy Award for Album of the Year in 1988, *Time Magazine* would go on to hail the album as the "greatest album of the 1980s." For all its critical and commercial success, the toll *'Sign O'the Times'* cost Prince wasn't lost on longtime engineer Susan Rogers, who left Prince's side in the studio following the LP's completion, recalling that "we spent more time and money on *Sign O' The Times* than anything he'd ever done. Much more work went into it...You were exaughsted, because this was a guy who'd work for 24 hours straight, then sleep for four hours, then work for another 24 hours...With Prince, music was all there was...We worked so many Christmas Eves and New Year's Days. It was compulsion, it was ambition, and it also filled a vacancy in his life." Prince's personal interpretation of the aforementioned vacancy seemed to redefine his work-a-holism more as a matter of necessity, wherein he felt so constantly a slave to his art simply because "I am music. I feel music. When I walk around, I hear brand new things. You're almost cursed. You're not even (its maker), you're just there to bring it forth. You know, 'Can't I go to sleep?' No. You can't. But OK, now you can. And you go to sleep, and you don't hear it, and then you're lonely. No one wants to be on Earth alone...The thing is that when you're called, you're called. I hear things in my sleep...My creativity is my life...Its guides my every day, my sleepless nights."

Prince...Evolving

"I'm one of the most bootlegged artists in the world."

—Prince

Chapter 17:

Black Album—1988

Coming off the wild success of '*Sign O'the Times*' with his creative license fully re-accredited by critics and fans alike, Prince next endeavored to enter an even more mysterious creative unknown with what became one of the most bootlegged albums in history, '*The Black Album.*' Recorded between September, 1986 and March, 1987, the Black LP was famously pulled off Warner Bros. release schedule in December, 1988 per Prince's request to label head Mo Ostin. For years to follow, questions over why Prince ordered the album shelved would fuel its black-market value as a must-have bootleg for many die-hard Prince record collectors, with *Billboard Magazine* for one example reporting that when "Prince pulled *The Black Album* weeks before its release…(he guaranteed) it near-mythic status. Urban legends spread like wildfire." In spite of the many theories that fans would bat around for years regarding the secrecy of the Black Album, its actual making was unfortunately not nearly as mysterious, with chief engineer for the album's recording sessions Susan Rogers, who explained that "I engineered all of the *Black Album*, except '*When 2 R in Love*,' " recalling that "the tracks were odds and ends, things we would do on a day off. When he was making an album, sometimes he wanted to break away and do something just to get it out of his system, like *'Le Grind'* or *'Cindy C'*... The Black Album was stuff he could do in his sleep. He didn't have to think about it. The 'one-on' funk stuff was so easy for him... So there were tracks that were mostly rough mixes and...that he never intended to release."

Another factor that appeared to go a long way to explaining his decision to pull it off Warner Bros. release schedule at the last minute was Prince's mood during much of the album's recording, which was definitely in line with the album's title, such that the artist himself later recalled that "I was very angry a lot of the time back then...and that was reflected in that album." Echoing his sentiment, Rogers further recalled that "he was in such a bad mood all the time and a lot of us were reaching a burnout phase with him...Many of us had been with him a long time, but we were further away than we'd ever been. As happy as he was with the Paisley Park studio, there was a feeling that things in his life just weren't right. It just wasn't a good feeling in the air and he wasn't as much fun to work with as he had been. I don't think he was very happy about his career at that point...(so) the Black Album came about as a result of some anger and desperation."

Prince's uncertainty about where to head in terms of the album's musical direction can be arguably heard in those tracks on the *Black Album* which feature the artist incorporating rap verses into his songs for the first time up to that point in his career, with engineer Susan Rogers explaining his motivation as growing in part out of "these discussions we'd have about whether rap was viable or not...He didn't really like rap, but he realized he had to address it in some way; though he didn't know how. He felt he was making *real* music and didn't like people who couldn't sing or attempted and were out of tune, (but) it was becoming obvious that rap was not going to be just a flash in the pan and that it was going to be a new movement." For his own part, Prince later conceded that "all this gangsta rap, I did that years ago...That's what I went through with the *Black Album*...I've gotten some criticism for the rap I've chosen to put in my past work. But there again, it came during my friction years... On the rap tip though, it is an old style and I have always done it kind of differently—half sung, you know, like *'Irresistible Bitch'* and some of the other things I used to do." Some of those tracks featuring rapping, including '*2 Nigs United for West Compton,*' '*Bob George,*' and '*Le Grind,*' Rogers recalled were recorded in one session for a birthday party planned later that evening for Shelia E, such that "he wanted to record some mindless party songs for her. Not too much thought went into them. He just recorded the tracks, walked over to Bernie Grundman's to master an acetate for the D.J. to play that night, and that was it. (They) were never intended for an album."

For the album's other assorted tracks, delving into some of their recording particulars, Susan Rogers began with a pair of tracks which featured Prince's continued experimentation with (vocal pitch-bending), featured prominently on both '*Cindy C*' and '*Bob George*,' recalling that "Prince often VSO'd the tape machine speed (used a varispeed oscillator) to achieve his characteristic high-speed vocal or guitar sound. He would use the VSO to turn down the speed of the machine while recording (meaning that the song would be playing in a lower key). When finished recording, he would take off the VSO, play the machine at normal speed, and have a track with a thin, high timbre. The other way of affecting the vocal was to use a harmonizer (Eventide Harmonizer H3000 or H949, typically) or pitch-shifter. For instance, the vocal on '*Bob George*' was achieved by feeding the signal into a Publison 'Infernal Machine' and pitch-shifting it down by an octave." When turning to the album's mostly programmed musical tracks, Rogers recalled that, in either case, "for live drums we would have used the Yamaha kit that Prince preferred then. The drum machine was the Linn LM1 that he used in the 1980s. For the album's keyboard tracks, Prince would have primarily played the Fairlight and Yamaha DX7. Where horns were present on the album, I liked using the AKG 414 mics."

When attention turned to mixing on what *Entertainment Weekly* would later call "audio murk," Rogers explained that "most of the '*Black Album*' tracks were recorded hastily, instruments may have been recorded at inconsistent levels, meaning that some instruments would be very compressed compared to others. It wasn't a deliberate choice on anyone's part." Elaborating from a technical point of view, Rogers recalled that "some tracks from the Black Album were mixed on the SSL at Paisley.

I know that we mixed *Cindy C* and *Le Grind* at home on the DeMideo console. I remember doing *Rock Hard* and *Two Nigs United*... at Sunset Sound (also a DeMideo console). Any SSL mixes, however, probably would have used the SSL compressor on the stereo bus and sounded very different from the DeMideo mixes."

When it eventually hit store shelves, critics had a love-fest with an album that Prince later referred to as "that angry bitter thing," with *Billboard Magazine*, in contrast to the latter critique, hailing the album as "brilliant, pure funk" that *Rolling Stone Magazine* further raved for its "crackling...James Brown horn licks, assorted grunts and groans (and) guitar leads that burned into your skull." That same publication would later report that "before its official release in late 1994, *The Black Album* became one of the most bootlegged LPs in pop history." Upon its official release, *Billboard Magazine* additionally praised the album as "a terrific little record that still delights, even after its mystique has faded." In spite of the aforementioned praise, Prince would eventually explain that, ultimately his decision to pull the album on December 8th, 1987, resulting in the destruction of roughly a half-million copies, arose out of the fact that "I suddenly realized that we can die at any moment... And we'd be judged by the last thing we left behind. I didn't want that... to be the last thing."

"He (Prince) hasn't lost his touch for inventive dance music... Thanks in large part to the seven-piece band with which he recorded the album...LoveSexy reveals how intricate and complex Prince's concept of funk has grown since 1980's Dirty Mind."

—*Rolling Stone Magazine*

Chapter 18:

LoveSexy—1988

Prince's answer to the *Black Album* would be a much more personally-enlightened affair: *LoveSexy*, with Prince, working at a truly-inspired pace, explaining that "I did *LoveSexy* in seven weeks from start to finish, and most of it was recorded in the order it was on the record...There were a couple of funky things I did at the end and put earlier on, but it's pretty much how you hear it." Fully free from the dark cloud that had hung over the sessions for the *Black Album,* with *LoveSexy*, Prince's former manager Alan Leeds detailed a creative epiphany in which he'd "had an awakening and made a major decision that he was gonna change his focus...He told us how (the *Black Album*) was the devil's work; that 'wasn't really me. I gotta make a record for God now.' This really was an epiphany. At that moment, this was a new guy. I'm not saying that his life changed dramatically, but certainly the music he made changed. His attitude in the studio changed. It was joyous music and he was enjoying making it." Elaborating further, Prince explained that, during the album's recording, he felt "good most of the time, and I like to express that by writing from joy."

Conceptually, Prince explained that the album was "a mind trip, like a psychedelic movie…(*LoveSexy* is) the feeling you get when you fall in love, not with a girl or boy, but with the heavens above." Musically, Prince explained his new band was "about musicality, a willingness to take risks," such that *Rolling Stone Magazine* was inspired enough to observe that the new material demonstrated "he hasn't lost his touch for inventive dance music…Thanks in large part to the seven-piece band with which he recorded the album…*LoveSexy* reveals how intricate and complex Prince's concept of funk has grown since 1980's *Dirty Mind.*" Delving further into Prince's conceptual mindstate throughout the album's recording, engineer Eddie Miller explained from his own first-hand observations during the album's recording that "I got the sense that he was going through some kind of change in his concept of sprituality. I also got the sense that his new girlfriend, Ingrid Chavez, had a significant influence on this change. She was definitely a 'new ager', setting up her set of crystals on the handful of sessions I got to do with her. I know Prince made some kind of public statement about why he shelved the Black album, but I don't remember exactly what it was. It was related to darkness and light, and he was going for '*Positivity*'. Lucky for me!"

Recalling the time-frame in which Prince began work on *LoveSexy* following his decision to shelf the Black album, Miller recalled that "I think a quick decision was made to start a new album (that turned into *LoveSexy*) in December. December 11, 1987 to be exact. I imagine Prince had his manager try to find a great engineer to start the album, but it didn't happen quickly enough for Prince, so I got the call early one morning (after just being home a few hours from the last session I did) to record Prince and the band. The band was rehearsing in Studio C, and Prince must have felt they were ready to record immediately. So Prince's live sound mixer 'Cubby' (Rob Colby—amazing engineer) who was running sound during rehearsal split the feed of the mics he set up and we ran them to studio B so I could record the band on 2 inch. It went smoothly—lucky for me! It was a sink or swim moment, and I guess I was swimming. Prince liked what he heard and I was off running on what turned out to be the first sessions for the *LoveSexy* record."

Continuing, Miller further recalled that "Joe Blaney was the engineer they were trying to fly in as quickly as possible from New York to start on this album. He arrived probably within a couple days of this, and since I got my foot in the door at the beginning, we played tag team engineers on the album. Joe was the experienced guy having worked with the Clash and a bunch of other bands coming into this project. I don't think that was really a secret to anyone, except I do remember Prince asking—about halfway into recording this album—he asked me what other albums I had engineered. I answered 'This is it', and he said 'Oh Shit.' I must have been doing a good job for him 1., not to immediately notice, and 2. , to have kept working with him steadily after that moment! A lot of sessions were just me and him, and it was really incredible. He was always in full performance mode in the studio, so it was like having your own concert. So even though I was getting paid $5/hour for at least half of the record (!!!!—even at that rate, I was making around $30k a year—you do the math!), I really didn't care. I would have paid to work there (being the biggest Prince fan in the world)! I knew I had been handed the engineering torch when I was handed the proverbial beeper. This was at a time when the only people who had beepers were doctors, and employees of Prince. No cell phones, so you had to call in from a pay phone when you were out."

Acting along with fellow engineer Joe Blaney as a co-recording team over the course of the album's studio sessions, Eddie Miller explained that "Joe was really cool to work with. Very easy-going, and very supportive of the work I was doing. I wish I got to work with him more, but like I said, we were playing tag in the studio, so I didn't really get to hang out with him very much. Prince had Joe start the mix for at least half of the songs on the album. And then Prince would come in, with my help, and deconstruct what Joe had going to put his own touch on it. It had to be weird for Joe—no one works like that! It was a big mish mash in terms of mixing. If Prince was coming in to do some overdubs, I would set up a working mix, and then who knows—maybe that would end up being the basis for what ended up being the final mix at the end of the night. That's the way it went. There was a period during the mixing of this album where about 4 different top engineers were flown in to take a stab at mixing songs on the album. I think the only mix of all those that partially made it on the album was started by Bob Brockman (who I went to school with at U of M!). He started the mix of '*Anna Stesia*', but then it was deconstructed by Prince with some help by me. When I say deconstructed, I mean that often these mixes that were started by Joe used the mix automation on the SSL console."

Revealing details about Prince's recording routine during the making of *LoveSexy*, Miller recalled that "Prince had a number of different recording approaches, all of which were employed on this album. There's the 'one man band approach' of which '*I Wish U Heaven*' is an example. The band approach, like on '*Eye No*' and '*Anna Stesia*.' The Prince starting with him playing live drums approach. The starting with drum machine approach. The band was very involved on this recording, unlike his 'Sign of the Times' album. Neatness wasn't the priority so much. You'd set everything up so that Prince could be behind the console and have everything at arm's reach. He'd run the tape machine unless he was recording guitar or doing something where he'd need another set of hands. So engineering with Prince was kind of an advanced assistant engineering gig a lot of the times. For the most part, Prince would record everything, including the vocals, and he'd have the artist replace the vocals he sang. I even think that his original vocals may very often have been erased (his decision!), although he kept rough mixes that were done with his vocals. Prince's technique in the studio as kind of an advanced porta-studio approach (popular 4 track cassette recorder). This was particularly evident with the recording done in the control room. You'd set Prince up behind the console so he could run everything himself, and whenever he could, he would. I understood that approach—you get rid of the middleman as much as possible so you can get straight to the music. It gets really tedious having to constantly ask the guy running the tape machine to "play", "rewind", etc., so why not do it yourself? Vocals were always done in the control room. Prince would generally kick everyone out of the control room when he was doing vocals. I'd just make sure that his mic was routed to a number of different tracks. He knew his way around the studio, so a lot of times, it was more like I was assisting Prince."

Elaborating further on the strengths of the band Prince had assembled for his new studio LP, engineer Eddie Miller concluded that "I would say that Prince's *LoveSexy* band may have been his most versatile band—especially in the 80's. The sound of that band wasn't too far removed from the Revolution, but they were lighter on their feet. Sheila was a perfect drummer for Prince. Prince was a perfect drummer for Prince. But Sheila can do anything, and she is so musical as a drummer—she really became part of the Minneapolis sound. Dr. Fink was probably the glue that kept the *LoveSexy* band rooted in the classic sound Prince got from the *Purple Rain* Era. Eric is to Prince like Clarence Clemmons is to Springsteen. I don't know if you ever heard 'The Family', but Eric was in that band, and I think it's a special album that was totally overlooked. One of the best albums to come out of Minneapolis from that era. That album had so many of the key elements that made Prince and the Minneapolis sound special—including lots of absolutely amazing Claire Fischer string arrangements, which were always my favorite (Prince's too!). Eric and I hit it off when we both realized that our favorite album was '*Native Dancer*' by Wayne Shorter (I think he's Eric's favorite sax player). That's another thing about the *LoveSexy* record. I think it might be the album that most captured a sense of all these different musical influences that Prince has. A lot of that had to do with his band at the time which between Sheila and Eric, they had a very legitimate claim to the jazz world. It's a difficult line to walk, because in the funk world, it can be too easy to cross the line over into sounding like a fusion band, or a smooth jazz record (to be avoided at all costs!). *LoveSexy* never did that, and I'd credit Prince's working style at the time for that. And his willingness to experiment on a record, to an almost avant-garde level. It didn't allow for things to become too slick—everyone was moving too fast for that to happen! Levi is just a solid/ quick musician, and I got the feeling he was the musical director when Prince wasn't in rehearsal. Miko really had the whole Prince funk rhythm guitar thing down, which would free Prince up to do lead guitar, or anything else. Matt and Eric were friends from way back as I remember, so they had their system down in their approach to the horns. It was interesting watching Prince and Eric come up with horn arrangements in the studio. Prince would sing a horn line to Eric, and then Eric would get it immediately, and quickly tell Matt what to play in terms of harmony and rhythm. Boom. *LoveSexy* captured Prince's most musically versatile band at a moment when everyone in the band was at the peak of their musical powers. Some of the songs were recorded with the band as the basis for the track. '*Eye No*', '*Anna Stesia*', possibly '*Dance On*,' which started with just Prince on drums."

Offering a more in-depth insight into the recording routine Prince ran his band and engineers through during the recording of any of the album's tracks, engineer Eddie Miller recalled that "Prince was tough on the band in rehearsal. If someone made a mistake, they were fined something like $50 (I think James Brown did this too). He had a sample of a cash register hooked up on a drum pad that he would hit if someone made a mistake (I'm sure James Brown didn't do that). I only had one bad night with Prince—and luckily I wasn't fined! It was probably set off by me taking an extra minute to hook up a mic or something, and I ruined his groove. The whole night was ruined from that point on, and it turned into a kind of Buddy Rich scenario, where Prince would threaten me all night saying 'I'd never work in this town again', or 'Don't you miss the weather in Miami (where I was from)'. Stuff like that. Not fun. But I only had one night of it. I think Susan Rogers had many years of it from what I heard. I was lucky. I think Prince was going through a kind of spiritual awakening at the time, so he was less apt to be in this kind of mood. I learned how to take 10 minute naps that were good enough to keep me going for days at a time. My sleeping patterns haven't been the same ever since." Offering an example via one of the album's specific songs, '*Eye No*,' Miller explained that "Prince walked in after doing the first take to listen to what was on a rehearsal tape from the band's jamming, I knew I was alright when he started dancing. I did have maybe an hour or so to get sounds while the band was rehearsing. I didn't have to worry about headphones for the band because Cubby had them set up with monitors, which in retrospect was a good thing sonically. I'm sure it beefed up the sound of the recording to have all the bleed through from the band being in one room with the monitor system blasting away. Prince did add a lot of overdubs to '*Eye No*' (A LOT!)', but most of the live band remained on the track. It may have been that Prince replaced a real bass with a synth bass from the band recording. I think it's also possible that the first take was the one that was used."

Once Prince had a basic template for any of the album's songs, Miller recalled that the idea in working with Prince wasn't to spend time getting a good sound, it was to capture the music on tape at the moment of peak performance. That's what essentially makes records sound good—to me at least. You have Prince as the main source, and it almost doesn't matter what kind of mic you put in front of him. But adding to that is the fact that he had about 3 or 4 techs on hand a good deal of the time (especially during the official time that *LoveSexy* was being recorded) to keep the gear working at its peak. Joel Bernstein was his guitar tech at the time, and he's probably the best there has ever been at the job. Brad was his drum tech—always tweaking up the drum tuning during most of the sessions. Matt Larson was his overall road tech—he'd set up the keyboards. Sal Greco would keep the studio gear running at its peak. The rooms and the consoles at Paisley Park sound great. I realized almost immediately that my basic job recording Prince was to keep the flow going, not spend time picking the perfect mic. A lot of sessions happened where I'd get the call that Prince was gonna show up at the studio in an hour. So the call would be sent out to the whole crew, and it was just a mad dash from my house to the studio, to throwing up some mics on the drums and getting Brad to hit them a few times. If I had time, I'd align the tape machines, otherwise Sal would often pitch in with that. I'd basically make sure all the rhythm instruments were ready to go, and a vocal mic. Drums, bass, a number of keyboards, electric guitar."

Atmospherically, Miller recalled a pace during the album's sessions wherein "Prince's concept of making a record was that 'it has a long way to go', so you really have to put everything you can into it. It'll cut through the noise of the day, it'll stand out from the competition if you really go all-out on every level. It's a great philosophy that I've tried to carry on in whatever I do. Everyone was on edge all the time at the studio because of the crazy unpredictable schedule, but that's the way he works. It must be to this day. As hard as I thought I was working, Prince was working harder. He really really worked hard to get where he is. One thing he would do that I never see anyone do is to videotape his performances, and then study them. It was his willingness to put himself under the microscope and address the problems he saw that got him to the level he's at as an artist. He rehearses his bands endlessly before they go public—for months and months—and they are top-notch musicians!. It doesn't just happen. I've worked with a lot of different artists at this point, and I've never seen anyone even close to matching his level of intensity and dedication."

Continuing, Miller explained that ahead of any recording session with Prince, "I'd try to check everything to make sure it was going to tape, and if I had any extra time before Prince showed up, I'd tweak the levels and eq, etc. But a lot of times things would happen so fast that I didn't even get to check stuff before he walked in. Not to mention that some-one would also have to decorate the studio to whatever degree possible, to give it some 'vibe' in the room. These changeovers happened quite often because Paisley Park was not only for Prince's use, it was rented out to the public, so a lot of times everything was torn down. Once we got into recording *LoveSexy*, we were able to keep things set up. And I wasn't sleeping because I wasn't only working with Prince, but I would assist almost all of the other sessions in both studios, for at least the first 6 months the studio was open—it was nutty. In that environment, you primarily have to make sure that stuff got to tape, and that you kept track of everything that was happening so nothing got lost. I did a good job of that, which I'm sure is why I was able to keep working with Prince for a good chunk of time. I'm also a musician (and a big fan!), which helped me to second guess what he might try to do next in the studio. The game was to try to be one step ahead on as many levels as possible, including making sure the coffee was fresh, the Doritos were on hand, and there was plenty of honey for the tea."

Detailing the studio set-up that Prince worked out of as he crafted the album, Miller explained that "Studio A had what's turned into a classic SSL 4000, and studio B had a custom API/Demedeo console that was moved from Prince's home studio. It didn't take long for me to realize how much warmer the API sounded. Both control rooms were identical in dimension and design if I remember correctly, so it was easy to draw a fair conclusion that the API sounded better. I believe Prince had the API designed for him based on a similar, if not exact console at Sunset Sound in LA where he worked a lot in the 80's." During recording, Miller recalled that "Prince didn't like the automation—it really wasn't intuitive because you couldn't see the faders moving. So if I was with him, he'd have me turn off the automation, and he'd/we'd manually move faders, stopping and editing the ½ inch we were mixing down to if a move was missed. I got my editing chops together very quickly. And in order to make mixing this way easier, Prince would record tracks with more than one dedicated item on it (say a keyboard part in the verse, and a totally different sound in the chorus) at levels that would make it easier to keep the faders at one level. Not really recommended for the best signal to noise ratio, but what the hell. Prince also didn't like syncing up two multitrack machines in order to get more tracks (too slow!), so some of the songs on *LoveSexy* had a whole bunch of different stuff on one track. '*Eye No*' comes to mind. It became very dense as the recording progressed. I had to really make sure that nothing was accidentally erased. And I think that's why I kept working with Prince. I tried to just keep the sessions flowing (and not erase anything!). Basic, but important stuff. Being a drummer, I had a good concept of drum sounds. That helped. I picked up some knowledge along the way, when I was awake enough. I remember one thing that really opened my eyes—very basic—was something Eddie Garcia showed me about getting a good kick drum sound. He'd use the GML eq to roll off a lot of the mid-bass, around 300 Hz to clear up the sound of the drum. Subtractive eq—what a concept."

As Prince built each of the album's tracks, beginning with a rhythm section that varied between a blend of programmed and live drums, with engineer Eddie Miller explained that the artist preferred "the Linn LM-1 drum machine, and three songs on *LoveSexy* used live drums. Two of the songs were recorded in the rehearsal room, studio C, and the mics used were split off of the setup Cubby had going for the live setup. I don't remember the mics, except I made a note that there was an RE 20 on the kick—although, the kick sound was replaced in the mix by a triggered sound in the Dynacord drum module. Joe recorded the drums for '*Dance On*' and '*Anna Stesia*'. '*Dance On*' would have been the same setup as '*Eye*

No', except Prince played drums on *'Dance On'*, and Sheila played on *'Eye No'*. Sheila also played on 'Anna Stesia', and the main sonic difference there was that the drums were recorded in studio A in the 'Stone Room.' Very live, dense, thick sound. But overall, there was nothing really out of the ordinary in how the drums were recorded, except for the extraordinary talent behind the kit. I think Sheila and Prince both primarily come from the same school of funk drumming, which is why Sheila is a perfect drummer for Prince. It's the Dave Garabaldi/ Mike Clark Oakland funk style—light on its feet, intricate ghost note—type style. 'Dance On' is definitely a Garabaldi influence drum pattern. I don't remember who it was that Prince learned some drums from early on, but whoever it was turned him on to this style of playing. And Prince is great at it—not easy to do. Sheila is a master. As a drummer, I was in heaven getting to work with two of the best drummers ever."

When attention turned to those keyboards Prince chose to lay down in the course of building *LoveSexy*, Miller cited "the Roland D-50, Ensonic ESQ-1, Fairlight, Yamaha DX-7, Roland Piano module (the piano on 'Anna Stesia') and an Ensonic sampler, he used the ensonic stuff a lot—it was fairly intuitive to use. I would say the D-50 was used the most, probably because it was the newest. I remember Prince saying that new keyboard sounds had an effect on giving him new song ideas. He also used the Dynacord drum module—triggered off tape, or off the linn. Kick drum from 'Eye No' was from Dynacord. Snare mis-triggering from *'Dance On'* was Dynacord. *'Glam Slam'* and *'I Wish U Heaven'* were dynacord kicks and snares." Continuing, Miller explained that "one of my main contributions to *LoveSexy* was getting Prince into sampling. It was something I had been into since college in terms of putting songs together entirely made of samples (I even put out an album of material like that called "Lecture on Nothing" Interestingly, it was released on a label called Pop Mafia Records that was owned by the engineer who recorded all of Claire Fishers string arrangements for Prince. His name is Arne Frager.) I figured out how to set up a keyboard triggered sampler that was quick and easy to use. It was a function in this expensive outboard box they had there called the Publison infernal Machine 90. The thing I liked about it is that you could easily get unity gain in and out of it, so that what you sampled off tape would go back to tape at the same level. It sounded good, and was quick to use for sampling. But I do think it opened up a lot of possibilities for Prince being able to quickly sample stuff—probably for the first time. He had a number of other samplers, but they weren't as quick to use, and speed was the name of the game in the studio with Prince."

Turning to the recording of Prince's guitar tracks, Miller recalled that "Prince had a handful of favorite guitars that he'd go to for lead parts, or for rhythm parts. His custom lead guitar would run into his pedal board in the control room, and then out in the room to his amp. I generally used a Senheiser 441 aimed a bit off center, and right up on the speaker. No compression, maybe a little eq sometimes. He has an Epiphone hollow body electric that he'd use for a super clean, warm sound. That would go through a D.I. right into the console. An example of that sound is on '*I wish U Heaven.*' That song was recorded and mixed in studio B on the API/DeMideo console. You can hear a difference in the sonics on that song. Much less compression than the songs mixed on the SSL. Definitely a warmer sound. Anytime we recorded bass, it was done direct. I think he had two basses he'd generally use: an Alembic (for his Stanley Clark 'Lopsy Lu' vibe), and a custom Fender P Bass if I remember correctly for a more straight up classic sound. And he has his great Telecaster." When time came for Prince to lay down the album's vocal tracks, engineer Eddie Miller recollected that "we used about three different vocal mics on '*LoveSexy*'. I do think that the lead vocal on '*Eye No*' was recorded live with the band, so that would have been whatever mic Cubby had for him for the live setup. The best mic we used was a classic U47 tube. The best mic pres in Studio A were a bank of outboard focusrites. So I'd generally plug the mic into one of those, and run it to an LA-2A, then to tape. For the first sessions I did with Prince, I set up a Neumann TLM-170. Not really a great choice, but I remember cranking up the E.Q. around 10k on the focusrite, and I think Prince liked the hyped nature of it. You can really hear that on '*Positivity*'. Any mic sounds good on Prince. I would say his voice is his best instrument."

Once principle recording for the album—over a record number of weeks—had been completed and Prince began mixing, Miller began by explaining that there was "no difference between tracking and mixing—we set up for both all the time. Most of the mixing for *LoveSexy* was done on the SSL—it had all the bells and whistles—meaning that an extensive eq, compressor and gate were built in to each channel. And I have to say that Prince really abused them when he got his hand on the board. Lots of the mixes on *LoveSexy* were really squashed using these SSL compressors. Mixes done on the API were less futzed with, mainly because it wasn't as quick to compress stuff, and there really weren't that many compressors in the room. In retrospect, that was probably the better way to go sonically. '*Glam Slam*' and '*I Wish U Heaven*' were mixed on the API. And you can hear the difference if you listen on the record (which by the way, the vinyl sounds way better than the CD). I don't think the cd has been remastered since the early days of digital in 1988—plus you don't have to fast forward to get to the song you want to hear (!)—while I'm on that, I asked Prince why he didn't want to put different index numbers on the cd for each song, and he just said 'It's all one song'. I pretty much understood the psychedelic implications of that."

Continuing, Miller recalled that "for mixing, a lot of times it was approached more like most people would do a rough mix. You'd have a working mix going on the console while tracking was in process, and if the vibe was good, Prince would just fine tune that pretty quickly and we'd print it onto the Studer 1/2" machine (30ips). A lot of people say they like their rough mixes better, but they don't have the cashews to release it that way. I think '*I Wish U Heaven*' went down that way. The working mix just sounded good, so Prince put it down that way. '*I Wish U Heaven*' was recorded and mixed in one 12 hour session. In that way, it's probably the most focused song on the album. All of the other songs went through a more extensive overdub process. The key sonic elements to that song were the Epiphone guitar, recorded direct into the API. The harp sample which I think came from the fairlight, with a repeating delay effect that we got from running it through a Lexicon PCM-42. The 'non-lin' AMS RMX reverb, and probably the 'ambience' setting on a second AMS reverb unit. We'd always have 3 1/2" machines ready to go, and the cassette deck (so Prince could quickly take a copy home or in the car to listen to). Often times after we finished a mix, Prince would immediately work on an extended mix of the song—while the mix was still up on the board. It would involve muting certain elements, and making edit pieces that you'd chop together. Prince would often add keyboards, etc. live on these edit pieces as they were going to the ½ inch machine. It was quicker than recording these new elements on 2 inch, but it made it all a one shot deal, because you couldn't then go back and remix the remix. The 3 ½ inch machines also allowed Prince to crossfade songs into one another, and add elements this way when it came time to putting the album together. *LoveSexy* all flows together as an album because of the editing that was done this way."

Of the album's controversial cover art, engineer Eddie Miller recalled that "at one point in an afternoon during recording, the photographer who shot the album cover (Jean-Baptiste Mondino) hung out while Prince was recording some overdubs—not something that happened very often. Later, Prince asked me about the *LoveSexy* cover. I said it was great, and he said that's why he liked me." Offering further reflections on Prince's musical state of mind throughout the album's recording, Miller began observing that "I think *LoveSexy* was a stepping off point for Prince in terms of the struggle he had to not get swallowed up by the music business. He mentioned that it was getting harder for him to make records the way he wanted to and *LoveSexy* was an attempt to regain control over his creative life. I think *LoveSexy* is one of the main albums Prince has made that musicians really gravitate towards. I don't think anyone is as successful as Prince is at bringing into a pop setting more complex harmonies and rhythms that are rooted in jazz. It's not so much that Prince is a jazz musician—it's more that he has big ears that allow him to incorporate jazz elements into his thing. Fortunately, I was good enough as an engineer, musician, and fan to be able to stay out of the way and let it happen. It also captured the sense of optimistic spirituality that Prince was discovering at the time."

Upon release, the album debuted at # 11 on the Billboard Top 200 Album Chart, and # 5 on the R&B Chart, producing the smash single 'Alphabet St.', which became a Top 10 Hit on the Billboard Hot 100 Singles Chart, with Prince for his part commenting years later in reflection that while "*LoveSexy* was supposed to be a failure...I've heard people say that record saved their lives." Critically, the reaction was—in fact—largely positive, with *Rolling Stone Magazine*, as one prominent example, wisely noting that "the most successful moments on *LoveSexy* prove that the hardest questions may not lend themselves to easy answers but make for much better music." Seeking to elevate his artistry to a new musical plateau—one which *Billboard Magazine* was inspired to term "a new phase of maturity," Prince himself explained ultimately, with *LoveSexy*, "either you went with it and had a mind-blowing experience, or you didn't."

"Batman is the Prince record many have been waiting for...(resulting) in the Minneapolis super-star's most mainstream accessible record in years..."

—*Detroit Free Press*

Chapter 19:

The Batman Motion Picture Soundtrack—1989

Picking up right where he'd left off with *LoveSexy*, Prince next dived head-first into the *Batman* Motion Picture Soundtrack, which Prince affectionately pointed out at the time as "the first tune I ever taught myself to play." Recorded on days off from the *LoveSexy* tour between mid-February and late-March of 1989, engineer Chuck Zwicky, who recorded the majority of the album alongside Prince, detailed a typically rigorous, work-a-holic routine wherein "Prince had an interesting schedule: he'd be on the road four days a week playing shows, then fly back to Minneapolis for three days over the weekend and pretty much record straight through, so we had quite a bit of 40-hour recording sessions in there." Echoing his fellow Paisley Park co-worker, fellow engineer Eddie Miller added that "Prince worked all the time. There was no routine or schedule. It was full steam ahead all the time. So as hard as you thought you were working, Prince was working harder. I remember stepping back and thinking how he had probably been on this type of schedule for at least the last decade before I had the chance to work with him. It was really unbelievable." Prince's chaotic schedule seemed to mirror that of the film's director, Tim Burton, with Prince recalling, following a visit to the set to discuss the soundtrack's musical blueprint, "there was so much pressure on Tim (Burton) for the whole picture I just said, 'Yes, Mr. Burton, what would you like?'" *Rolling Stone Magazine* would indeed later observe in its review of the album that "Prince's *Batman* soundtrack is packaged as songs written for the movie's characters."

Using the film's dailies in real-time as literal inspiration in the studio during the album's recording, engineer Chuck Zwicky recalled that "for the recording of the Batman record, at the studio, we had a video monitor up on the wall above the studio window so Prince could watch rushes of the movie that Warner Bros. would send him, with a note 'This is the scene, we want a song for this.' Prince—most effectively at that time—was kind of an iconic figure, and he wasn't arrogant about it, but he enjoyed the anonymity that it gave him in the studio. He was basically given a very hands-off freedom to craft the film's songs, and having worked with a lot of film composers, and knowing the kind of reeming they get from directors and editors, where they are constantly re-writing and re-conforming, and not so in this case. I've worked with a lot of different producers in my life, and I probably appreciate Prince's process more than anybody else's, because he sort of becomes a part of what he's experiencing. Of all the producers I've ever worked with, I've never seen him second-guess himself or scratch his head. He kind of gets what he wants to get out of what he's seeing and applies it with his own style. Prince is an incredibly hard working writer, and he is constantly in the studio recording new songs, and coming with his notebook and works till he has a song, and is very quick and very determined about it. Prince is entirely conceptual when he's writing lyrics, and would write some amazing fiction, great stuff, and would create these interactions and scenarios and characters; it's sort of what makes his music fun and is all very imaginative. Probably for me, the best part of that experience, came with a sense we all had of what that film meant, how the rushes were looking, you really got a sense of this kind of dark mystery this film was going to represent. So that concept really fueled his creative imagination, the idea of this sexy underworld vibe that was going on. So that was very inspiring for him." Elaborating on his creative process in the course of crafting the album, Prince explained a creative philosophy/ process wherein "one thing I think is important is that one learns how to listen. So I never stop being a fan. Even if the music was coming through me, I was still listening to it as an admirer of the sound, so whatever I heard, be it a lyric or a melody line or a beat or whatever, sometimes just the bass line, I paid attention to it, and I would let that start the song first. Once you get that main thing down, then that's the leader and that's gonna tell you what the next instrument is supposed to be."

Expanding further on his own observations of Prince's writing style(s) during the course of the album's recording, fellow Paisley Park engineer Eddie Miller, who engineered the recording of '*Electric Chair*' among other Prince recordings during the Batman era, recalled that "he would write all sorts of ways. I have to admit that I listened to some of his cassette demos that he would sometimes bring into the studio to reference (as I remember, he would hold the cassette player up to his ear, so you couldn't really hear it.). They were fascinating. His cassette demo technique was extremely crude but ingenious—it's like something you'd do if you had no access to any equipment. He'd use two cheap cassette recorders. If he wanted to hear drums, he'd record a human beat box rhythm for the length of the song—and most likely, he'd have the form of the song in his head while he was recording this. By the way, it was the same in the studio when he'd do his one man band approach to recording a song. He'd know the song in his head, and start out recording the drums for the song (it would essentially become the 'click track'—the way a click track should be). Back to the cassette demo—he'd then play his beat box groove over the speaker on the cassette recorder and sing the bass line while recording all this onto the second cassette machine. He'd build up a rhythm track this way, and then add vocals. And there's your demo. I imagine it's a technique he developed probably in high school to be able to easily put his ideas together without getting hung up at all with the recording process. I actually heard a tape of an entire album fleshed out this way."

Returning with the *Batman* soundtrack to a one-man band in the studio from *LoveSexy's* group recording approach, engineer Eddie Miller—who worked with Prince during this era—reasoned that in watching Prince work in the studio while also having the demands of the *LoveSexy* tour simultaneously to juggle, "it was quicker for Prince to record everything himself than to have to worry about getting more people involved. I think he had so much music in his head that the most important thing was to get it down on tape while it was happening." Chuck Zwicky, who served as the soundtrack album's primary engineer, next explained that once the pair had entered the studio, "the one thing about working with Prince—or any artist who is that prolific and that determined—is that they have a very specific way they like to work, and it's very efficient for them. When I was working with Prince, I was interested in speed, repeatability, and efficiency. He just did not want anyone who was fussing over gear, he nicknamed a particular engineer 'Groove Killer' because he'd fuss around over stuff. With Prince, everything—with the exception of live drums—was recorded in the control room. The Batman soundtrack was all done at Studio A at Paisley Park, the studio was an SSL 6000 E, and the 24-track tape machines we used were Studer A-800 Mark 3s. All of Prince's parts were recorded in the control room, and he was basically outfitted with every instrument hooked up, ready to go on tape at any point within an arm's length. So he'd set up a keyboard or guitar next to the auto-locator, which is the remote for the tape machine, right in front of the console, where he'd have a boom mic hanging a microphone right in the middle of the console, set of headphones, a headphone amp, and behind him on the equipment rack would be his drum machines and his guitar pedals that he ran the drum machines through. So he kind of had his own little world and knew instinctively where everything was. He was very consistent in how he'd lay out his tracks—it was just consistent—he could sit there at the console, reach his hand over, push up a fader and say 'I need a bass for this,' and he'd know exactly what he expected to hear on each track. The other thing that was remarkably consistent for Prince is that track 1 on every 24-track master of Prince's was always for the handclaps. It was as if one of the only separate outputs he'd take from the Linn was for handclaps. He had, in the past, printed a few different instruments on there, but due to tapes being mangled, he'd gotten really frustrated by that, and so he decided never to have anything on track one that was more important than handclaps. Also, you don't get as much low end on track 1 or 24 of a tape simply from fringing effects, which means the tapehead sort of sprays onto the tape, and it has margins on either side of any internal track, but an edge-track only has a margin on one side. So track 1 was always handclaps, track 2 was always kick drum, track 3 was always snare, and track 4 was a mono-output for the drum machine routed through all his guitar pedals. That was it—if it wasn't live drums that was it—every record you've ever heard of Prince with a drum machine, from '*When Doves Cry*' on, is 4 tracks of drum machine, and all the flanging and other effects you hear are all printed to tape through guitar pedals. You'd know that track 9, for example, was always the bass guitar, and that track 16 was always the lead vocal, and tracks 17 through 24 were always background vocal parts."

Along with original compositional ideas Prince was churning out in the course of crafting the *Batman* soundtrack. Engineer Chuck Zwicky also explained that Prince derivatively drew on his own unreleased catalog from the legendary Vault for inspiration, recalling that "one of most interesting jobs I had was going into the vault to mix songs that had never been mixed, let alone released. So in a couple of weeks, I'd mixed like 135 songs that were just sitting, that he wanted to hear. I think he wanted to do a retrospective because some of these tapes were as old as 1978; so that was very interesting to go through all that, because the process involved getting all the tapes and first making sure they were playable. Back then, there was no chance of using automation, because there was no time code on any of the reels, so we did all the mixes manually and very quickly on a single pass through. In the case of the vault mixes, they were done by me totally unintended because he was on the road touring *LoveSexy*. In that era, sitting at an SSL console in 1988 was a pretty cutting-edge experience, the console was—and is still—capable of some really tremendously articulated sounds that earlier generation stuff wasn't gravitated toward. So one of the most interesting aspects was to be able to do a mix of something that he had recorded 10 years before; and in many cases, I wasn't even familiar with, it was stuff that he had subsequently given to other artists to record. So occasionally some assistant or runner would walk through and go 'Oh, that's on this or that record...' So in that case, I'd stop mixing, but it was always interesting to hear those studio people comment 'Oh my God, it sounds really punchy and huge, and not like the early 80s record that it was.' So I was taking things pretty much at face value, at least in terms of what they represented musically, and Prince would listen through them. I remember throughout our working on the *Batman* record, he would hear a certain piece of something, and ask 'Can you get that tape back up here, I want to sample that string part off of this,' so he may have figured the Batman thing as a different kind of project—not collaging—but in terms of his identity as an artist. It was the first time he was pretty much composing music for something he wasn't starring in. So that's what was happening around the beginning of the Batman album, I think he was digging around and listening to what he'd done and getting a bigger picture in the process of who he was as a process."

In building any of the album's 9 tracks, Zwicky revealed that Prince often began with the drum track, explaining that "his working process at that time was to come up with a pattern on the drum machine, and if there were to be fills—going back to the fact that Prince recorded very consistently: claps, kick, snare, drum mix for the first four tracks. They're always patched in, they're always set, and the levels are always set. He'll come back to a track, and decide 'This needs to have a break here,' and he'd go in and put the snare track of his pre-programmed drum machine in record, record, erase several bars of it, play a fill manually on the pads of the drum machine, then punch himself out. And you'd be sitting there thinking 'Wow, there's no going back from that, because there's no way to synch up the drum machine, no synch tone, none of that.'" Continuing with a technical detailing of the drum machines Prince worked with in the course of recording the album, Chuck Zwicky recalled that "Prince had a collection of LM1 Linn drum machines—which were the first generation of Linn drum machine, and had first come out around 1981, cost around $7000 and he had 6 or 7 of them. And he had a second generation hand-clap chip in it, the original hand-clap chip is considerably more spikey and scattered than the tighter one he got, which he'd often tune down to get his massive Prince hand-clap sound. When we started on Batman, the LM1s were all out on tour, so out in the tech room in the basement of Paisley Park, they had a lot of road spares. So I managed to go down and scrape up enough parts to put together a couple of working LM1s, but they would have various problems like buttons wouldn't work or outputs would have no signal, and eventually there was a bit of a panic because he was coming back off tour to record. So we tried to rent one, but nobody in Minneapolis or Minnesota had one—so we ended up renting a different drum machine, the Linn drum, which was the second generation of the LM1, and is considerably a sounding machine. So listening to the Batman soundtrack, you can tell that's not the Linn drum. The Linn drum, apart from the LM1, had quite an interesting difference: the tom tom samples are much longer. The tom toms on the original LM1 are very, very short. Back in 1981 computer memory was very expensive, so everything was kept very very short. So for instance, if you listen to the toms on '*When Dove's Cry*', which are these little thuddy sounds, versus '*Scandalous*', the toms are much longer in their sustain because they were recorded on the 2nd generation Linn. Also, by that time, he was triggering a lot of samples from a Dynachord ADD1, which was a drum-trigger module that had drum samples in it, and he was triggering those inputs from the audio outputs of the Linn, and you can hear those all over *LoveSexy* and on Batman songs like '*Electric Chair*,' —they were all triggered from that box. After *Sign O'the Times*, he got the Dynachord ADD1 module, which is a large, 3-4 rack white-painted module with grey lettering, and he was triggering most of the kicks and snares on *LoveSexy* and several on Batman were triggered on that box."

Elaborating, engineer Eddie Miller, who also worked on the *Batman* album, further explained that "when we recorded a track using the Linn, he would manually add fills as the track was being recorded—he thought of the drum machine in that way like he did when he was playing drums—meaning that he'd have the song in his head when the drums were being recorded whether he was playing them, or using the Lynn. He also used the Dynacord drum module, which triggered kick and snare sounds for many of the songs. Prince also used the LM-1, which had 4 outputs for clap, kick, snare, and a mix of everything else that would run through a number of guitar pedal effects. The effects are what gave Prince his own Linn sound, along with the 'non-lin' AMS reverb. I suspect it was either Susan Rogers or David Z. that helped set up that scenario with him." Continuing, primary album engineer Chuck Zwicky recalled that "there were a bunch of interesting things that happened on that record, one of them being a Publison Infernal Machine 90, which had a sampler built into it, sort of like the AMSS sampler where you could grab snippets of audio. But the Publison also had a pitch-shifter, so he could hook up a keyboard, play a line he'd sampled off tape, and play it in a different key. So he did a lot of sonic manipulation with that box, that sampler played a huge part in his production style at that time." Elaborating further on the synthesizers Prince utilized in the album's production, Zwicky detailed that "one was a Roland D50, a digital synthesizer and the EMU Emulator 2 or EMAX 16 sampler, one of those two, we also had a Fairlight that sat in the corner, and once for some Simmons Tom Fills and once for some handclaps. He always had Sonic, Emax, Emulator 2, and the Roland D-50 were the main keyboards Prince played on the *Batman* record."

While much of the album's music was electronic-based, engineer Chuck Zwicky explained that "because I was dealing with a synthetic environment at the time and being a fan of real instruments, I wanted to make sure there were a few real instruments on the record. I was a big fan of Prince's earlier records where he'd play live drums and the standard Fender jazz bass, and so I'd always try to make sure some of those instruments were around in the studio, and if possible, asked somebody to dig up some of his old instruments. For instance, at one point I did dig up his old telecaster, that Hohner copy, and he looked at it and laughed, and I think he felt he was doing a record that was a bit more future-driven, and didn't want to rest on his laurels." Expanding his recollections of Prince's recording process for the album's guitar tracks, Zwicky recalled that "back then he was using primarily his custom-made cloud guitar, which was always strung with really light strings, like 9s, and lots of fingerees all over the fingerboard, plus his fingerboards were laquered, so you'd pick up that guitar and it was very slippery. So that was his deal. It had EMT pick-ups, and was usually run through a ton of Boss pedals, and was very much his rock guitar. As far as guitar pedals went, in those days, the guitar pedal business was not nearly the way it is now, there were not that many custom-made or boutique pedals, and in the interest of productivity, Prince is a great example of an artist who epitomized: it's not what you use, but how you use it. His guitar pedals were the most run-of-the-mill, generic Boss pedals… there was nothing special… the only thing he had that was slightly special was a Colorsound Wah Pedal,. At that time, it hadn't been reissued and was somewhat hard to find, and had a very distinctive sound and very distinctive travel compared to a Crybaby pedal, which he'd also used."

When attention turned to the album's vocal layers, Zwicky began by recalling that, related to the album's broader instrumentation, "one really cool thing we did vocally on that record in an effort to create a solo effect involved him singing into an SM-57, and we'd bring up a transformer, patch it through some of his guitar pedals, distortion and Wawa pedals and things; and he'd basically sit there and scat-sing, and it would come out sounding like some weird synthesizer solo, or even a guitar." Continuing, the engineer—in commenting on Prince's vocal recording process—revealed that it "is remarkable, he does it alone and does every vocal as he's always done sitting down in a chair at the console, at the mix position, with headphones on, and just pulls a boom mic over to where he's sitting right in front—say it's dangling between the speakers and he'll pull it towards him—and he'll sit there with his lyric sheets in front of him, the remote control for the tape machine under one hand, lights dimmed, and no one else in the room. And you sit and wait to be paged when he needs you to punch in something or clean something up or move something or create a track for him to record an additional part, or something he's not comfortable doing like that. Other than that, he basically layers the vocal parts on himself."

Detailing Prince's mic preferences during the album's vocal sessions, Zwicky recalled that "there were two microphones we primarily used on that record, because the last thing you want is a problem with a vocal mic on a Prince record. He had this great Neumann 47 we used on some songs, but after some questionable noise issues or intermittent power supply issues, we ditched that for a C-12 for leads and a 57, which we used for a lot of the effect solos where he'd sing through guitar pedals. Also, on one occasion, we used a TLM-170 Neumann. When tube mics were getting a little noisy or crackly, we'd switch to a solid-state mic. A lot of the vocals were cut straight through the SSL. On occasion, when we were listening to a mix he'd decide there's a vocal line where I want to change something, and being overworked, underpaid, and sort of really stressed out you're thinking 'Oh good, I can go sit in the lounge for a few minutes and relax,' and he turned to me in this particular instance and said 'No, wait, just wait here,' put on his headphones and proceeded to replace an entire section in the middle of a verse with a four-part harmony. That, to me, was an example of the fact that there aren't a lot of other singers out there like him: he's really got a great imagination for what he creates vocally, and if you were to listen back through some of the multi-track vocal parts on that record, and soloed up any of those tracks—because remember he never really bounced tracks down, he'd keep tracks 17-24 reserved for backing vocals. And if you soloed up any of those tracks, you'd swear there were eight different people singing, because he'd create characters."

In context of the film's characters, when Prince found a dialogue sample he wished to use as part of one of the album's songs, *'Party Man'* for instance, the engineer explained that "we had video tape machines plugged into the video monitor he'd be watching the rushes on. And if Prince found a character's line he wanted to sample into a song—then we'd run an output from the videotape they would send—either putting them into the Publison to sample—or flying them other ways onto the multi-track. Those voices were taken directly from the actual Warner rush video cassettes, and Prince would sample them into whatever song we were working on." Addressing the recording process for some of the album's individual tracks, engineer Chuck Zwicky began with the LP's opening song, *The Future,'* explaining that "on *The Future's* rhythm track, you'll hear a Boss (envelope) filter, a Boss overdrive, the orange one. And all that percussion is simply Tom Tom hits and other percussion sounds—a cowbell—going through those Boss pedals and onto tape, that's what makes that weird percussive effect. On that song, the guitar parts were played a semi-hollow 335 that had humbucker pickups on it, not EMTs. I mentioned the Publison, a harmonizer that had the ability to record and then trigger the sounds back, and the guitar sounds at the end of The Future, for example, are just sampled off tape, and then Prince would play the Publison running his fingers up and down the keyboard that was triggering it. So that was Prince running his fingers up and down a keyboard playing back a sample of a guitar lick he'd recorded previously, a lot of weird sounds like that."

Turning attention to the album's second song, engineer Eddie Miller recalled that "I worked on the *Batman* album on '*Electric Chair*,' which was probably the best sounding recording I did with Prince, but maybe I think that because of the great mix that Chris Lord-Alge did! I do remember Joel Bernstein saying he loved the guitar sound, and that was about as high a compliment that I've ever had. We built the drum track using the Linn, which had 4 outputs with guitar effects on the 4th track. The typical reverb/ effects setup for the song was this: 1 short reverb (usually the AMS RMX 'non-lin' setting), 1 long reverb (usually another AMS RMX set on 'Ambience'), harmonizer panned right (an AMS DMX set for no delay, but pitched up 1.007 or so)— maybe Susan showed me that, or Prince told me. For '*Electric Chair*'—the potluck send I set up happened to be in tune with the song, so it became part of the sound. I set up a potluck reverb before the session started—a kind of ring modulator setting in the Eventide 2016 used on snare."

Expanding to the recording of the album's biggest single, '*Bat Dance*', which reached #1 on the Billboard Top 200 Pop Singles Chart, engineer Chuck Zwicky recollected a serendipitous process wherein, prior to the start of the song's recording, "we had also recorded a couple of songs with Sheena Easton, which Prince had written for Sheena, which had a very Marilyn Monroe vocal delivery—very sexy—and Prince came to me and asked if I could put a tambourine on the song. And when I asked what he'd like to hear, he said '16th notes, something like that, I'm going to go home and take a bath. Can you do it?' And I said 'I know exactly how I'm going to do it,' and he said 'I don't want to know how, just do it.' So he left and later called me up from his house and asked 'Did you put the tambourine on? Can you mix it?' So when he came back to the studio a couple of hours later and wanted to hear the mix, he asked if I could put the tape back up. And as I was playing the song with the tambourine mixed in, he went digging around for the tambourine, and then asked 'How did you do that?' And I said 'Well, when we recorded this, I wrote down on the track sheet what the tempo was, and then went to the Linn drum and programmed in a tambourine playing that pattern, then sampled it into the Publison, then routed the kick drum into the Publison; so every time the kick drum got hit on the downbeat of a measure it would trigger the 16th note, and keep re-triggering it so it would stay locked to the kick drum."

Continuing, the engineer recalled that "now Prince is looking at me like it's sinking in, and asked 'Can you do that with any sound?' And I said 'Yeah, you can take anything off tape and trigger it, you can take a bass line, a guitar, repeat anything and just repeat that bar if you want.' So on the beginning of Batdance, when you hear that bass line come in, and then the kick drum, it's because the kick drum's triggering that bass line from the Publison, which we sampled off tape. He played the bass line on the synth all the way through, which was played on either a D-50 or an EPS-16, which is in Sonic. So the Batdance all came about from that episode of me putting a tambourine part on a Sheena Easton song he'd written, and then his triggering that bassline. And a lot of the rest of the Batman soundtrack is based a lot on that technology, which is one of the reasons it doesn't sound like other Prince records." Expanding on what he felt made the album's rhythm section stand out from past Prince projects stylistically, engineer Chuck Zwicky explained that "I remember we had a break over Xmas in 1988, and I flew out to San Francisco to visit my sister, and her husband gave me a T-Shirt as a gift from a house club he worked at called DV8, that had a Pirate's smiley face on it, as was the norm in 1988. And it said 'DV8—Acid House,' and so after the New Year, I wore it to Paisley one day, and it caught Prince's attention and he asked 'Where did you get that shirt?' And I told him where it was from, and he replied 'Yeah, of course it's not here in Minneapolis,' and at that point, he was pretty interested in House music."

When working on Vicki Waiting, which *Billboard Magazine* hailed as "an excellent pure pop song," Zwicky explained that the song was constructed using the "Dynachord drum machine being triggered by the original Linn LM1 drum machine, and for keyboards, he played the Roland D50 and EMU Emulator 2." For 'The Arms of Orion,' a duet between Prince and Sheena Easton, which became a Top 40 hit in both the U.S. and U.K., Zwicky—who recorded the song—revealed "an interesting recording story where Prince called me in and wanted to know if there was an electric piano around the studio, and I scrambled because I wanted to make sure there was something real around instrumentally. So I remember scrambling—knowing he was coming in soon to record—to find an electric piano, a Rhodes, or preferably a Wurlitzer, and we found a Wurlitzer in the basement, and it was kind of a bitch to get the thing working without some sort of buzz happening. But we managed to set it up, and so the piano to that song was played by Prince in the control room on a Wurlitzer model 200 electric piano. He programmed his drum machine, and we recorded about 7 minutes of drum machine, then sat down at the Wurlitzer with the lyric sheet in front of him, and got the structure and recorded that, and then embellished it with various synthesizer overdubs. He used a C-12 to record his vocal for that song in the control room, and when Sheena Easton came in to sing 'Arms of Orion,' we put her out in the studio to sing. Prince spent a lot of time coaching Sheena on that vocal, over the course of several intense hours, because he's so specific about what he's going after that he's not insecure about it; therefore he's not harsh or short-tempered about it. He knows what it's going to take to get what he needs out of it, and knows he's dealing with talented people like Sheena. For instance, I remember Sheena asked a lot of questions about how he wanted things to go, and she'd give him examples, and he'd say 'More like this,' and sing it back to her. There were also sections where they were singing in unison and octave, so she'd have to match the vocal he had on tape. They wrote the lyrics together, and I remember Prince had his lyric notebook open and he didn't know what Orion was, and she explained it was a constellation and drew a picture with the two arms, and they fleshed out the lyrics from there. She was really great to work with."

Debuting at #1 upon release, as *Billboard Magazine* reported, the album "spent six weeks at the top of the charts," selling 4.5 million copies, and producing the hit singles '*Batdance*' (# 1) and '*Party Man*' (#8) among others. Batman brought full circle the restoration of Prince's status as one of the world's marquee pop superstars, and critics roundly hailed the album as such, with *Rolling Stone Magazine* beginning the chorus of praise with its conclusion that the album "starts and ends with some of Prince's most radical funk," while Prince's hometown newspaper, the St. Paul Pioneer Press, noted that "*Batman* gives Prince new structure, focus...(with) tightly arranged and densely packed with a broad range of sounds...(he has produced) an album that could well stand as the new high point of Prince's career." Q Magazine, for its part, hailed the album as "Prince's most cohesive work since 1999," while the Detroit Free Press concluded that "*Batman* is the Prince record many have been waiting for...(resulting) in the Minneapolis superstar's most mainstream accessible record in years...You can hear the Boy Wonder say it: "Holy hit singles, Batman! Prince has done it again!"

> "*Batman* was all about that same feeling. Graffiti Bridge was probably more about that feeling than LoveSexy was. LoveSexy was a state of mind I've come to, and I know it is still there... If I didn't have it, I wouldn't make records anymore. When you have that...you know who you are, and you know what your name is. I didn't know that before. I thought there were places I had to get to. I thought there were things I had to do. I was a lot more competitive because of it. Now I realize that's not what's important."
>
> —Prince, 1989

"The album folds musical experiments in with the beat. Since the mid-1980's, Prince has been toying with harmony and texture, seeing how many eccentric add-ons he can get away with. Songs sometimes grew too wispy and cute in the process, but now he has found a balance."

—the *New York Times*, 1990

Chapter 20:

Graffiti Bridge Soundtrack—1990

Building off the wild mainstream success of the Batman Soundtrack, Prince next expanded his musical foray into the soundtrack universe, beginning work on the ensemble soundtrack album to this third feature film, '*Graffiti Bridge.*' Though primarily performed and produced instrumentally by Prince, the album boasted a cast of vocal guest-stars that *Rolling Stone Magazine* praised by pointing out that by this point in his recording career, the artist had "long proved that he can credibly emit any sound, from orchestral lush to Beatlemaniac cute, Prince forgoes his outré style tinkering to fix on rock and funk, pumping the latter with neat guest spots by George Clinton on '*We Can Funk*' and by Prince's resurrected R&B protégés in the Time on '*Shake!*' Gospel veteran Mavis Staples shines on the strutting '*Melody Cool.*'"

While clearly impressed by the album's collaborations, the magazine seemed even more dazzled with the fact that "most of the album is Prince solo—his guitar soaring from crunchy Steve Cropper-isms to baroque Hendrix frenzy, his studio smarts peppering tracks with enough hand claps, keyboard peals and artful noise to keep the listener, in this day of texture-happy production, consistently surprised and intrigued." Echoing Rock's biggest music publication, Prince's hometown paper, the St. Paul Pioneer Press, seemed eager to point out that while the soundtrack's guest-star roster was impressive, "it's Prince's genius and astonishingly far-reaching talent that hold it all together," and while the *New York Times* for its part, noted that "while he may be pop's most sought-after collaborator," *Entertainment Weekly* was quick to clarify that ultimately Prince "can create a world so overpowering that a song sung by someone else can still be his."

Explaining that "half the songs we recorded during the Batman sessions ended up on his next album, the *Graffiti Bridge* soundtrack," album engineer Chuck Zwicky, who worked prominently on both records, added the appropriate context to both projects in terms of Prince's typically tireless work ethic by recalling that—on days off from tour—"when I worked with Prince, he would come to the studio in the morning, between 10 AM and Noon, then rehearse with the band until 6 or 7 at night say, go home, have dinner, come back and record till 3 or 4 in the morning, go home and watch the videotapes of the rehearsal from that day. Then get up the next day, rehearse 6 or 7 hours, go into the studio and record for 6 or 7 hours, go home and watch 4 or 5 hours of videotapes—the same thing, day in and day out. People have no idea what a sacrifice that man made to be Prince, he spent every waking hour either rehearsing, recording or studying the rehearsals."

Commenting for his own part on his aforementioned commitment to craft, Prince mused at the time that "people call me a workaholic, but I've always considered that a compliment. John Coltrane played the saxophone 12 hours a day. That's not a maniac, that's a dedicated musician whose spirit drives his body to work so hard. I think that's something to aspire to. People say that I take myself too seriously. I consider that a compliment, too." For a musician who spent as much time working in the studio as Prince conceded he did, engineer Chuck Zwicky clarified that the time was not spent laboring over any single song or sound, revealing that "Prince is one of the few producers I've worked with who never second-guesses himself or scratches his head, but beyond that there's a certain element to his personality that I really understand and appreciate: he kind of knows in a very precise, non-verbal way what it is he's going for and what he's going to achieve, and it makes it seem almost other-human, he's not going through the normal questioning process most artists do, and if he does, it's always internal. On that record, and in general when recording Prince, we would pretty much put everything to tape as you hear it, there was no cataloging of what to do next. It was done or it wasn't, basically. One thing about Prince was: if there was a problem, he wanted to deal with it instantly, so we generally would mix a song as soon as we recorded it." Elaborating further on an up-close look at the artist's gift for instant perfection in performance during the recording of Graffiti Bridge, fellow album engineer Michael Koppelman explained that "Prince was a great musician, it was just obvious working with him. I remember at one point where he was playing something, and he wanted me to play a few notes on the lower end of the keyboard, so I came over, and I said 'You want me to hit that 7 there,' and he laughed at me and said 'Oh, you're one of those that read music.' I'm sure he did to some degree, but he had no idea what a 7th was in terms of music theory, which is something fairly basic when you're trained in music, you learn these intervals. So even though he was completely untrained in music, Prince had a great, gifted ear, and I'd say he could sit down with anyone in any genre and pretty much hang with them naturally, pretty much out of pure talent. So that was always fun to watch him."

Principally recorded at Paisley Park Studios, Zwicky recalled that the first songs he and Prince worked on for the album came "one period during the *LoveSexy* tour where Prince had flown back for one of our 3-day recording sessions over a weekend, and we had rented this Linn drum because our in-house Linn was broken, and we ended up recording 3 songs, all 3 of which session all ended up on *Graffiti Bridge*. One of those was '*Elephants and Flowers*.' When we finished that one, I felt like 'Oh my God, I finally feel like I'm involved with a Prince hit.' It was a great song. When I set him up to record the vocal on '*Elephants and Flowers*,' he called me back in after he was done, and said 'I'm going to go take a bath,' which was often where I'd start to mix. And I was listening to this track thinking 'Wait, where did that guitar come from? We didn't track a guitar, that's amazing,' and I'm going through the tracks, and I found the acoustic guitar on the lead vocal track. So he'd been sitting at the console, with the vocal mic in front of him, strumming the acoustic guitar and singing on one track. He played a big acoustic Guild maple guitar for that session, and the U-47 vocal mic was up for that session. So Monday morning, 10 AM when Theresa came into the studio, I'd been there since Friday afternoon, and Prince had recorded and mixed 3 songs in that time, and was just exaughsted. So I hand her the notebook and headphones, and she says 'What is that for?' And I said, 'You're not coming in to write down the lyrics?' And she said 'What lyrics?' And I said 'For the songs we recorded?' And she replied with surprise 'What songs did you record?' And so I said 'We recorded 3 songs,' and showed her the list. And she said 'What are you talking about? Prince didn't record this weekend, did he?' And I said 'Yeah, we've been in here since Friday, and haven't been home since.' And she said 'He didn't sing, did he?' And I said 'Yeah, we got 3 songs done,' and she said 'He's not supposed to singing, he has strep throat. He's supposed to be home resting.' And I said 'Oh my god; that would explain it. I thought he was doing a Bob Dylan impression on *Elephants and Flowers*.' Because his voice is really rough, and she said 'No, he has strep throat, and is supposed to be resting to get back on tour today.' Another song from that session was '*The Question of U*,' which he sampled a Claude Debuse record on that song."

When he wasn't on tour, fellow album engineer Michael Koppelman— who came to work at Paisley Park following the release of the *Batman* album—recalled that "during *Graffiti Bridge*, Prince was in very sort of a hermit kind of a stage, where all he did was work, he didn't party at all, he wasn't going to L.A., none of that kind of stuff." Elaborating on his own introduction into Prince's musical universe, Koppelman recalled that "he had started working on *Graffiti Bridge*, and myself and all the other assistant engineers were doing lead engineering sessions for Prince at Paisley Park. And there was sort of a friendly competition going on, no one knew if Prince was looking for another engineer or what. So

I remember one day we were trying to mic up a drum, and there were two of us in the room with Prince, and Prince looked over at me and said 'None of you guys here can mix.' And I said 'You've never let me try to mix something,' so he said 'Alright, you wanna try and mix this?' And he handed me '*Can't Stop this Feeling I Got*', and I stayed there all night mixing the song, made him a cassette, drove it over to his house in the morning, and slipped it in the front door. So he called me the next day and said 'Sounds cool man!' Then he brought me back in and we finished the mix, and that was sort of the beginning of how I became one of his new lead engineers."

For both of the album's principle engineers, the process of recording Prince was a similar one in which, as Michael Koppelman recalled, "he'd come to the studio with an idea all done in his head, and sometimes he'd have a little demo tape of him singing by himself or playing guitar or piano, but most of the times he wouldn't have anything. He'd just walk in and tell you exactly what he was going to do, then do it all himself all in one day, so the song would be basically done by the time he went home." Delving more in-depthly on what made that sort of precision possible, Koppelman continued, explaining that "when I started working with Prince, for the most part there was no room for opinions, early on; and when I'd first started working with him, the way he worked was: you'd get every possible instrument set up in the studio, then he'd just kind of point at something and go, 'Okay, give me the bass,' and then pick it up, and when he pressed a note, he expected a sound to come out. We had the track armed, it was routed there, so things went very fast logistically like that. So when I first started working with him, you were just kind of the help and just trying to make things happen that were supposed to happen that he wanted to happen."

Elaborating for his own part on the rare occasion where Prince would require the assistance of an engineer's opinion, Chuck Zwicky recollected "several occasions where he'd ask 'What's that?' And I'd explain as briefly as possible—because he hates explanations, and I remember once when somebody came into the room and had asked me a technical question, and I started explaining in nuanced-detail, Prince cut me off and said 'Chuck doesn't answer questions, he conveys information.' "

Expanding further, fellow album engineer Michael Koppelman shared that "at the beginning, when he was working, he might make an off-handed comment, but when I first started working with him, he was just very intolerant and expected everything to be done perfectly right now, and he sort of purposely strikes fear in people's hearts along those lines: not accommodating, not nice, not friendly. But over time, he used to call me into the studio, and he'd say 'Hey, have you seen this movie' or 'Have you heard this record?', where we would just talk about stuff." Regardless of how long Prince had known or worked with any of his studio staff, engineer Chuck Zwicky recalled that "stardom has never interfered with the work, and there was never a moment when he would pull rockstar on you."

Describing the technical layout of Studios' A & B, where Prince recorded the majority of *Graffiti Bridge*, engineer Michael Koppelman recalled that "Studio A at Paisley, which has an SSL Console and 2 Studer 24-track analog machines, I think everything we did back then was on 2-inch analog. Studio B at Paisley is a handmade board, a very idiosyncratic one, but a great sounding console, and Prince had used it in his studio prior to moving into Paisley. So he worked out of both of those rooms, but most of the work was done in Studio A. In terms of outboard gear used on the album, we had 2 DVX compressors, and Focus Right EQs and Mic-Pre's, a lot of DPI mic-pre's that we used in those days, some Neves, so we had a lot of outboard pre-amps that we used." Continuing, he explained that "Prince's head tech at Paisley during that time was a guy named Matt, and so he and his guys would go in the studio and set up everything—the drums, guitar amps, guitars, basses, they'd bring in all the keyboards into the studio, the racks, and get all that set up."

Once Prince entered the studio to begin working, engineer Chuck Zwicky detailed a creative process in which "I've seen him sit down with his notebook and write out lyrics, go out to the drums and sit down with the lyrics on the music stand and lay down his drum track, then come back into the control room and put down the rest of the parts. He's a very prolific writer, and one of the greatest psychological tools Prince had at his disposal was that: by the time a record of his was released, he already had 3 or 4 more in the can. So he was ALWAYS in writing mode." Elaborating, engineer Michael Koppelman recalled from his own observations working on Graffiti Bridge that, in the context of Prince's writing process, "There were times when we'd work on songs when it was obviously just some moment of inspiration." Offering a specific example of the latter process in action, Koppelman cited the album's biggest hit single, '*Thieves in the Temple*,' which reached # 6 on the Billboard Top 100 Singles Chart, explaining that "we did that in one long day. That was one of those where he came in with an idea, ready to go, and I remember we started at some point during the day, Prince and I worked all night, and I left the next morning along with him. I got called back at 2 or 3 in the afternoon, and Prince had ended up coming back an hour after we'd both left in the morning, and called in another engineer, Tom, who continued to work with him on it all day. So by the time I got back and picked back up working on it at 6 that night, Tom left, I kept working on it, and they shot the video for it the next day. I remember that we mixed it, handed it to Prince, he handed it to the video folks, and they began working on the video that same night."

Addressing those derivative influences which Prince referenced in the course of mapping out *Graffiti Bridge*, Prince's hometown newspaper, the St. Paul Pioneer Press, pointed out the fact that the artist "blatantly and affectionately tapped into rhythm and blues, gospel and blues, at the same time incorporating bits of rap and hip-hop." Translating how that latter fact came to life in the studio, engineer Chuck Zwicky explained from his own observations during the recording of the album that "the way that Prince's music comes together has everything to do with how he views the individual instruments, and for example, when he's sitting down at the drums, he's derivatively thinking about Dave Gerbaldi, the drummer from Tower of Power, and that's a real fascile and funky drummer; and when he plays keyboards, he's thinking about James Brown's horn player, on one aspect; and when he's playing guitar, other elements creep in, because he loves Carlos Santana, and Jimi Hendrix, and this other guitar player named Bill Nelson, a rock guitar player from the 70s. And so these aspects all come together to make this unique sound that is Prince, and it's not rock, it's not funk, it's not jazz, it's not blues—it's just his own kind of music. I remember there was one particular moment when he started playing this keyboard line, and I'm thinking 'He can't play that, that's Gary Newman.' And at that moment, he stops the tape, and turns and looks at me and asks 'Do you like Gary Newman?' And I said 'You know, the album Replica never left my turntable in Jr. High School after my sister bought it for me. I listened to it until it wore out.' And he said 'There are people still trying to figure out what a genius he is.' "

Once principle tracking had begun, attention first turned to tracking what *Time Magazine* concluded were "bass and drum sounds…(that) are absolutely engulfing. Musicians and producers are likely to pore over this record, scratching their heads and wondering how he does it," and that the *New York Times* more specifically highlighted in terms of the "hard-edged drum-machine beat…(that) paces *'New Power Generation'* and *'Elephants and Flowers,'* while short, percussive sound-samples ricochet through *'Tick, Tick, Bang!',* and the wistful *'Round and Round,'* … (with) its deep, lurching drumbeat and guitar riff…Prince isn't copying hip-hop—he doesn't try to outtalk or outstomp rappers—but he has clearly paid attention to it." Elaborating the discussion of the specific synthesizers and samplers Prince utilized in the course of recording Graffiti Bridge, engineer Michael Koppelman began by explaining that "the Midi-keyboard side got more elaborate as time went on, but when I first worked with Prince, he used no Midi, but he had keyboards like a C-50 and a Emulator Sampler, but none of it was Midi, and not something we'd synch to tape on anything." Where many of the album's rhythm tracks were programmed using The Linn drum machine, LM1 and the Dynachord ADD1 drum modules, engineer Chuck Zwicky recalled that for "there were a couple of songs on that record where he did play live drums, and when we were tracking, first off, the drums were always impeccibly tuned by his drum tech Brad, and he set up his drums in a really interesting way: with an extra tom to the left and right of the high-hat and snare. I usually miced his kit with KM84 or 67 mics on overheads, we also used TLM-170s."

With his rhythm tracks laid, Prince in any given song's recording sessions, would next turn his attention to the guitar's, with engineer Chuck Zwicky beginning by pointing out that "if you listen to his guitar tracks, on that album and others, there really isn't a lot of rhythm guitar tracks per say, there might be some funk guitar licks in there, but the thing about Prince's arrangements is their kind of insidious, they don't really come fully-formed, they're little bits and pieces that add up. So his rhythm guitar parts are very sparce, he's not strumming the chord changes and saying 'This is the back-bone of my tune.' When Prince picked up the guitar to record solos, he would definitely work up a lot of arrangement ideas. You're dealing with a guy whose got a great compositional sense, and so when he picked up the guitar, he didn't just noodle till he hit on an idea, he would get into the track and if it was working, you'd hear it, and if it wasn't, he'd get rid of it. He doesn't waste his time."

Continuing, the engineer explained that "I had an interesting conversation once with Jerry Leiber, of the Leiber and Stoller songwriting team, who back in the 50s and 60s wrote a bunch of Rock & Roll hits, including Elvis Presley's '*Hound Dog*' and '*Jailhouse Rock,' 'Stand By Me,' and 'Yakity Yak'* among a bunch of others. And I was working with his son, Oliver Leiber, who produced Paula Abdul's debut LP, and the Corrs and Sheena Easton among a bunch of others, and he and I produced some stuff together, and one day I was at his father Jerry's house, and I asked him 'What was it like in the 50s?' Because his son and I would work for a week on a bass overdub on a mini-moog, and Jerry said 'Back then, we had four hours, and that was the session; that was the union limit on a session. We'd try to record four songs in that time, and the musicians thought we were assholes because we pushed them too hard. But if a bass line didn't work, we'd get rid of it. We didn't have time to fuck around like you guys do.' And in no small way, that's kind of the school where Prince is from. He doesn't come from the school of laboring over parts in a song. If you can see something in its entirety, and you know where you're going with it, you know exactly what parts are there and what parts are missing, and someone whose not so exposed to the writing or creation process would think these things were being snatched out of the air. So he'd sit with a guitar, work out some parts on tape as it's recording, and that was the song, because he basically had the facility on the guitar—and every other instrument—to bring the song to the level it needed to be."

In terms of specific equipment, engineer Michael Koppelman recalled that "for guitars, Prince had his Honer Tele-looking thing, and other than that, it was a variety of different guitars the guys would set up. Because there were times when he'd have in mind using a certain guitar for a certain song." Elaborating on his set-up during guitar tracking, engineer Chuck Zwicky recalled that "I'd sit there with him, and he'd be sitting in a chair at the console playing, usually with some amps miced up out in the studio, usually with around 3 mics set up. He had a lot of Mesa Boogie cabinets, not just the 1 by 12, but a lot of the larger external cabinets. So he had the Mesa Boogie head, and then for his clean tone, his live rig wasn't direct, it was a set of JBL 12-inch speakers with a Crown Solid-State power amp driving them. At Paisley studio A, we had the large live room, and then a small stone drum room which is modeled after the drum room at Townhouse, where Phil Collins was recording a lot of his stuff at that time. And a small, wood room with very high ceilings, and so I usually put the guitar amp in that wood room, because it didn't have such a live ambiance as the stone room, and yet wasn't completely dead. So I remember putting a Senheiser 441 on that amp, a Crown PCM taped to the wall for ambiance, and something a little more hi-fi close to the cabinet, usually a Neumann TLM-170 or something like that."

As Prince began his vocal recording process for any of the album's songs, engineer Michael Koppelman recalled that "when Prince recorded vocals, when we could, we almost always used a C12 Tube mic, there was 247 that we used from time to time, but with Prince, almost 100% of the time we used this special C12 that had been modified and had a new membrane or something. The Prince vocal chain to tape was the C12 to the API or Neve or Focusright Pres, and then through that GML EQ, and then I usually use the 160X compressor coming back on tape. Going to tape, I like to use something a little heavy-handed, a Tube compressor. That was a typical vocal chain. We also had all the normal tools, a couple like plate reverbs at Paisley that we'd hook up every now and then, but most of it was the state-of-the-art digital gear of the time. We had these GML EQs at the time, which were really nice." As with guitars, Koppelman explained that "when Prince would track vocals, he'd kick everyone out of the control room, and we'd have hung his vocal mic right over the board, and he'd do all his own punching and sing right over the board. So you'd basically get him set up with the headphones and a mic, then leave, then he'd stay in there for sometimes a short time and sometimes a long time, so when he'd get back to you hours later, the vocals would be completely done, the backgrounds would be completely done and multi-tracked. Sometimes he'd call me in to move them around, so like if he'd layered up one chorus, we'd move that around to the other choruses,,, stuff like that."

Expanding further, the engineer revealed that "the big thing that Prince did back in those days, in the pre-sampler era, was the Publison, which was this sweet sampler that could change the pitch without changing the time—in real time, and at the time it was a hugely expensive box—$20,000 I think. Anyway, it allowed Prince to sample a vocal, then play a harmony on the keyboard. He did that TONS, so during the *Graffiti Bridge* and *Diamonds and Pearls* era, the Publison rules—Prince just used that on everything. You can hear it, if you pay attention, that there's a lot of sampled harmonies going on, in vocals, but not just vocals, with all the instruments, he would move around with stuff like that. That's how he'd move stuff around, if you put the backgrounds on the first chorus, we could move them to the other choruses with the Publison, because we weren't synched up like Midi or anything like that, and didn't have any other link source. So we leveraged the hell out of that Publison, it was like his main tool in those days."

Exploring the specific recording process for some of what *Rolling Stone Magazine* deemed "a seventeen-song tour de force that reclaims Prince's rare stature as a pop Picasso," beginning with '*Joy in Repetition*,' which *Time Magazine* praised for its "experimentation...(which) is to be expected from a true musical visionary like Prince. And...it pays off, as on the mysterious jazzy mood of '*Joy in Repetition*." The *New York Times* equally hailed the psychadelic masterpiece for its "surreal...arrangement that evolves cinematically, with instruments and sounds floating in and out like wisps of smoke." Engineer Chuck Zwicky, who engineered the track with Prince, recalled that "I recorded '*Joy in Repetition*,' and as a producer, I do a lot of atmospheric and trippy-sounding stuff, and I've always loved that sort of thing, and remember back then I used to spend a lot of time setting up effects. On the SSL console, there were four aux-sends we used, that is an echo send, and they'd all have the same basic four effects on them: a long reverb, a short reverb, a harmonizer that's not pitched in any way; it's just flat and panned to one side so he can make it stereo, which is like a little delay, and a vocal delay. And I used to set up some things that were very evocative, and one of my favorite reverbs from that era that we used on that song among others was the Lexicon PCM 70, which had a bit of a difficult user interface at that time. It was just a simple one line florescent display with two rows of buttons, and no real indication of how many parameters were in there. You'd have to page through things to get to that, but once you got into that box, you could control an awful lot of things about the way you could make a reverb do things, that no other reverb could do. This included some very very spooky, almost out of tune, haunting tones, and I used to love those sounds, and would set them up and instead of using the AMS RMX 16 long ambience program for a big reverb, I'd set up this Lexicon, and when you'd turn it up, and turn into this magical kind of floaty thing. So he'd turn aux-sends and hear something different like that, and used it in that song, and some others on the record." Of '*Round and Round*,' which starred guest-vocalist and Prince protégé Tevin Campbell and reached #12 on Billboard's Top 40 Singles Chart, engineer Michael Koppelman recalled of its recording that "I remember Prince recorded Tevin Campbell's vocals himself, and sort of kicked everybody else out."

Of another of the album's dreamier leaning sonic epics, '*Still Would Stand All Time*,' which *Entertainment Weekly* praised as a "deep, profoundly original song of shivery musical explorations sung in a simple, direct gospel style," engineer Chuck Zwicky explained that "I recorded that for the *Batman* record, and we'd just finished the record, and had edited together the final sequence, and at the last minute, Prince changed his mind—and it was one of the few times he asked for my opinion for something as major as this—but he said 'I want you to put up this one and this one, and listen to these two songs, and tell me which you think goes on the Batman record.' And the songs were '*Scandalous*' and '*Still Would Stand All Time*,' and he says 'Well?' And I said '*Scandalous*,' and he said 'Oh, okay,' and then as with a lot of times, he paused, and the curiosity would get to him, and he said 'Why?' And I said 'Simple, it's Sexy.' And he said 'That's all I need to hear.' " Continuing, Zwicky recalled that "*Still Would Stand All Time*' has a sample off of one of my Claude Debuse orchestral compositions called '*The Afternoon of a Fawn*', which we sampled and slowed down, for a string break-down in the middle. I remember when we were flying it in, right before the flute melody, he stopped me and said 'No, no stop there, that's the hook, right before the flute melody comes in,' and it was so funny to hear him describe this motif in a classical piece as a hook. But he's right, it was the hook, and there's other parts on the song that are Clare Fisher's string parts that were just sampled off another record he'd done for Prince. There were no strings hired for that session."

Elaborating further on the album's string sections, fellow Paisley Park engineer Michael Koppelman revealed that Prince had a secret ally in orchestral composer, who Prince had worked with since the *Parade* album, that "Clare Fisher, this composer from California, Prince for some reason trusted this guy completely, and never edited his strings, so he would send a song out to him, and Clare would track the string arrangements, then send them back completed. Prince never met him, and felt it was working so well he didn't want to fuck with it. Then he would sample the shit out of the strings on other stuff. We'd basically listen through and grab out strings and then play them back on other songs. Most any time you hear Prince songs with strings on them from that era, it's from his work with Clare Fisher." Elaborating further, fellow PP engineer Eddie Miller recalled that "I remember telling Prince how much I loved the arrangement Clare would come up with and Prince told me that he was just in awe of the guy. Prince said he never even wanted to meet him, it was like some kind of magic thing that would happen when Prince would send a song off to Clare—he didn't even want to talk to him. Clare is like magic to Prince, and I understand."

With a 17-song opus that ranged from string arrangements to subtle hip-hop elements, which Prince would more aggressively introduce into the musical fabric of his next studio LP, 1991's '*Diamonds and Pearls*,' back at the turn of the decade, engineer Chuck Zwicky explained that for those moments where rap appeared throughout *Graffiti Bridge*, Prince's interest in the genre rooted from "an element of 70s glam that appealed to him about that hip-hop movement. Around that time, George Clinton was in the studio, and I think he saw that, and so the *Graffiti Bridge* soundtrack was trying to get into a bit of that too—the whole street culture thing—and I think it seemed a little dated at the time that it came out." Elaborating more in-depthly, engineer Michael Koppelman recalled of George Clinton's influence where it might have also tied into and contributed to the presence of hip hop on the soundtrack, "Prince obviously respected him a lot. The song they did together for that record, '*We Can Funk*', is kind of a blur because George would come in and out of our studio at various times while he was working on his own record at Paisley Park, and on that song, I remember Prince basically let George screw around on that track. So Prince left, and George ran the show a little bit in terms of putting some of his musicians on the track. We used the C-12 mic."

Released on August 20th, 1990, '*Graffiti Bridge*' debuted at #6 on the Billboard Top 200 Album Chart, going platinum soon thereafter, and inspiring a chorus of critical praise that began with *Rolling Stone*'s observation throughout the album of "a sharper focus and harder groove... (that raises) *Graffiti Bridge* above the reckless genre dabbling that often enlivened but sometimes undercut *Parade, Around the World in a Day* and *LoveSexy*...with *Graffiti Bridge*...Prince reasserts his originality." *Time Magazine*, meanwhile, determined that "all in all, *Graffiti Bridge* is a groovable feast of an album (17 songs), loaded with exotic dishes... many of the songs are excellent." Prince's hometown newspaper, the St. Paul Pioneer Press, for its part, concluded that "with the assurance of a master, Prince has reasserted his reputation as one of pop's most brilliant innovators with his new album, '*Graffiti Bridge*,'...An artistic triumph... he delves from his trademark tight, funk-rock groove deeply into black musical roots...As always, there's plenty of energetic funk-rock, which, along with tight, multi-textured arrangements and Prince's production finesse, ties it all together." Finally, *Entertainment Weekly* proclaimed that with the album Prince was "back with a double album that seems like a masterpiece...It's clear from the very start that Prince has done something both impressive and essential...He's covered more stylistic ground than most musicians manage in a lifetime."

Prince...of the World

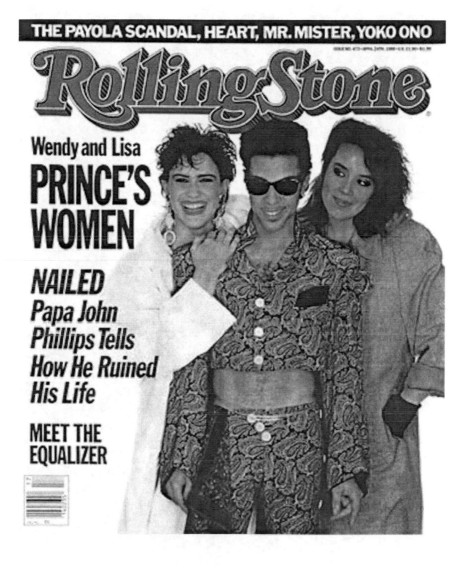

THE PAYOLA SCANDAL, HEART, MR. MISTER, YOKO ONO

Rolling Stone

Wendy and Lisa

PRINCE'S WOMEN

NAILED
Papa John
Phillips Tells
How He Ruined
His Life

**MEET THE
EQUALIZER**

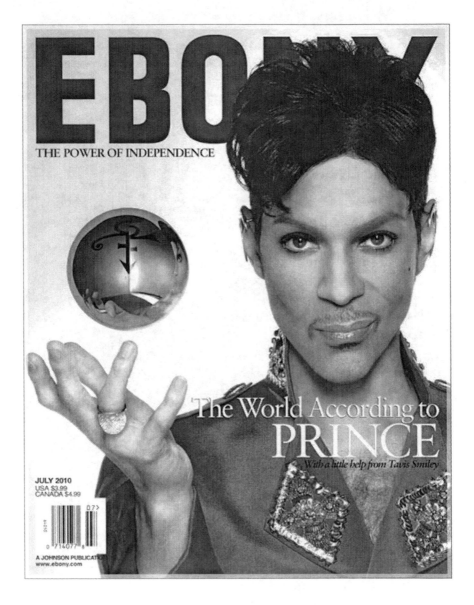

*"All my last records...have been connected to films.
This is just my music... I just wanted to tell you
how long we took making this."*

—Prince

Chapter 21:

Diamonds and Pearls—1991

Prince, like any pop superstar with career longevity, had always survived
by his hits, and with '*Diamonds and Pearls*,' the superstar was clearly
aiming for the stars, in synch with his record label, with Jeff Gold,
Senior V.P. of Creative Services at Warner Bros., recalling that his—and
Prince's—bosses at the label, "Mo Ostin and Lenny Waronker, had
decided they were going to get Prince to make a great album, not just
a good album...They felt his career needed a boost again." To reclaim
his throne atop the pop charts, Prince decided to sink a much lengthier
investment of time into the production of the album, explaining at the
time that "all my last records...have been connected to films. This is just
my music... I just wanted to tell you how long we took making this."
Engineer Michael Koppelman, fleshing the latter time-frame out more
indepthly, recalled that "*Diamonds and Pearls* was my main baby when
I was working at Paisley, and I remember we cut that together from
roughs and demos around Christmas, and the record wasn't done for
like 14 months thereafter."

Among the other changes Prince was making in the course of revamping his approach to record making for the 1990s was forming his first official back-up band since the Revolution with the New Power Generation, composed of Levi Seacer Jr. on guitar, Sonny T on bass, Tommy Barbarella on Keyboards, Rosie Gaines on Back-up Vocals, and Michael Bland on drums, with holdover Eric Leeds continuing on horns. The group, musically, was as dazzling a band as Prince had been on his own in the same right for many records past, such that critics including *Rolling Stone Magazine* praised the band for living up so precisely to that musical legacy, commenting in their review of the LP that "the album introduces the New Power Generation, which proves fully capable of jumping from the sly garage rock of '*Cream*' to a light ska groove in '*Willing and Able*.' Drummer Michael B. is an especially impressive anchor, helping give *Diamonds and Pearls* the most band-oriented sound of Prince's career." *Entertainment Weekly*, meanwhile, noted positively along the same lines as RS that Prince's "use of the New Power Generation is a major step…in what could be seen as a way to help conjure the old magic." The Detroit Free Press, for its part, noted of the album that "all of these songs are tightly written, affording just enough air for Prince's latest band, the New Power Generation, to insert the most distinct group imprint of any Prince album…NPG gives it a different kind of cohesion, an expansiveness that treads into sonic areas different from those Prince has traveled on his own."

Prince, for his own part, seemed equally delighted, praising "the wonderful people I have working with me. They keep me energized." In elaborating on why he opted to return to a live-band recording format, Prince explained that, in the course of seeking a more organic sound, while "everyone else went out and got drum machines and computers, so for this album I threw mine away…I think that I'm constantly changing. One thing I notice is that some people want me to play like I used to play, and what they forget sometimes is that I was there. I did it, so for me to do it again is not gonna be so exciting. If I'm going to play '*Let's Go Crazy*,' then I don't want another song that sounds like that, because I've got that slot filled. I'm always trying to look for something new… What was important was what came out of my system that particular day. I don't live in the past. I don't play my old records for that reason. I make a statement, then move on to the next."

One thing that stayed the same in this process was Prince's musical bar, set as high as ever, with drummer Michael Bland explaining that "(Prince's) demands on me were exactly the same as his demands on himself. There's no separation. He only wants to work with people who have the same work ethic he does. On a daily basis he's switching things around and organizing and writing new music. He's made me very unaccepting of slackers." Echoing the latter was world-class back-up vocalist Rosie Gaines, who recalled that "Prince makes you want to work…You had to get used to sleeping three hours, having nine hours of rehearsals, and if you were lucky you got lunch." Of the powerful boost to the NPG that came with vocalist Rosie Gaines, which proved a personally special addition for Prince, Levi Seacer Jr. recalled that "when Boni (Prince's back-up singer) left the band to go solo…Prince was reluctant to take on anyone new. He didn't want someone who would up and leave. With his music, you need to feel like family, real close. But I knew Rosie Gaines from San Francisco. I had been in a band with her, and I persuaded Prince to listen to her sing Marvin Gaye's 'What's Going On?' He couldn't believe what he was hearing."

Elaborating further on how profoundly impressed Prince was with his new back-up singer, album engineer Michael Koppelman recalled that "Prince adored her as a singer and a person too; she's very lovely and easy to adore. She could sing her ass off and Prince had enormous respect for that, and she was someone who could turn it on like a switch, and Prince could call her into the studio at any time for anything, and she would always surprise him with what she did. I would call her a first-take kind of singer, I don't recall us ever having to work hard to get anything out of her." For her own part, Gaines recalled that upon joining Prince's band, he "made me feel good about myself…Prince taught me so much. He took a month or so to get to know me, but we became very close. We would go for drives and he would play me music. Diamonds and Pearls was the best time for me." Prince was clearly in awe of the singer, commenting at the time of her vocal prowess that "Rosie…is like a tornado. There's never enough hours in the day for her voice. There's never enough tape for her voice...(I've) waited seven years for this."

In addition to the latter line-up, Prince—in an effort to add an urban edge to his revamped sound—added a goof-ball rapper named Tony M., inarguably the group's weakest musical link in a collection of other-wise stellar players, as exemplified by *Rolling Stone*'s commentary in its review of the LP that "less successful are the attempts to integrate rap into Prince's pop universe...(It) sounds like an obligatory effort, including a genre with which Prince has never been comfortable...A verse or two by N.P.G. rapper Tony M. in *'Willing and Able'* is...fine...but giving him an entire song —*'Jughead,'* a silly attempt at a new dance craze—is simply a waste. Tony's rapping style, also featured on 'Push,' is functional, but his rhymes are insubstantial." *Entertainment Weekly* further noted in its otherwise-positive review that "Prince's concession to changing times is to insert the deep-voiced raps of Tony M. into several songs, which makes him seem a trend follower, not a trendsetter." In explaining his decision to add the latter member of the NPG, Prince was experimenting with a re-invention of sorts, with album engineer Michael Koppelman recalling that "during this period, he was looking for this bigger, badder, harder sound, and was listening to that kind of music—like rap music, and really in your face, loud music, and wanted to be musically *hard* like that. I remember we would have conversations about it, and I don't remember how it came up, but one day I recall us having a conversation about rap and the origins of hip hop, and I said 'You know, in some ways, you sort of invented rap,' because he was playing around with all of that before even Run DMC. And I remember him agreeing with me when I said that, like 'Yeah, I guess I kind of did in some way of defining it.' " Elaborating further on Prince's musical motivations for incorporating hip-hop into his sound, longtime horn player Eric Leeds further offered that "for years, everyone was listening to Prince to see what he was doing, but there came a time when he began listening to rap and said 'I can do that, and I can do it better." Adding his own reflective commentary, NPG rapper Tony M. added at the time that "I think black awareness is really taking an upturn today...and he really wants to be a part of that."

In re-inventing his sound for the 1990s, Prince explained that, philosophically-speaking, in taking his time to record the album, "I feel that music is a blessing. I don't feel like I'm working. So when I'm not 'working,' I'm thinking about it, so music takes up a good portion of the time." From the artist's vantage point, his being so musically thorough had always been among the secrets of his genre-defining success, with Prince reasoning that, in context of the results he achieved, "you know when you buy someone's record and there's always an element missing? The voice is wrong or the drums are lame or something? On mine there's nothing missing." In spite of the new band line-up, one thing that hadn't changed about Prince's record-making process was his prolific nature as a songwriter, such that his engineer Michael Koppelman recalled at the time that, heading into principle tracking, "Prince sketched together *Diamonds and Pearls* very quickly, so I'd say within a few weeks we had something very similar to the finished *Diamonds and Pearls* done. It was a combination of stuff from the vault, and stuff he demoed very quickly, and then we spent a year and change after that working on it after that, but the main songs didn't really change. It was just the detail." Further explaining why he worked at the frantic pace he often did as a songwriter, Prince explained at the time that "I make music because if I don't, I'd die. I record because it's in my blood. I hear sounds all the time. It's almost a curse: to know you can always make something new…I work a lot. I'm trying to get a lot of things done very quickly, so that I can stop working for a while. Everyone's afraid I'm gonna die… I walk around and go to the bathroom and try to brush my teeth and all of the sudden the toothbrush starts vibrating! That's a groove, you know… You gotta go with that, and that means drop the toothbrush and get down to the studio or get to a bass guitar, quick! My best things have come out like that."

Still, in spite of how quickly he'd written the songs, given what he had commercially at stake, Prince was working at a much more methodical pace on the recording of '*Diamonds and Pearls*,' a process he kept very close to his vest, with engineer Michael Koppelman recalling that, as a result, "he never would have articulated his goals for any album with me, even at the end, I was still sort of logistical help for the most part. He did all of that totally himself, and you never really knew ahead of recording what his plans were. I remember when we cut that first sketch-up of the album together, I said 'This is a great record!' and we were fired up about it, but I think we had no idea of how far away we were from releasing it at that point." Delving into Prince's typical process for tracking on the album, Koppelman began by explaining that "But most of the time, he worked on one song at a time. The normal day at Paisley was we worked on one song, there were a lot of exceptions where we'd track sometimes when he'd have his band, the New Power Generation, in the studio with him. In those instances, we'd set everything up and they'd track a dozen songs or more and jam and screw around. Then Prince would work on those sessions for months or years afterward. Within those 14 months, we'd record some songs completely from scratch, and build others up from what was existing. In terms of when he recorded all the instruments himself vs. recording with the band, there were certain songs in his repertoire what were band songs to him, and some that just came out of jamming in some cases, and in most of those cases, it just seemed like he had a small idea that he just played around with the band until it was done versus having something preconceived in his head. There were a few times I remember him working on specific parts with people—like Tommy Barbarella when he was playing keyboards, I remember times when Prince would be over there showing him exactly what to play. With keyboards, a lot of times that's what you need, but with the other guys who were in the band when I was there—Sonny on the bass, and Michael on the drums, and Levi and those guys, he didn't have to tell them anything. They were just total pros all the time, they could just play their asses off all the time. So for Prince, I think it was fun for him to sit around and get inspired by those guys just doing their thing. For instance Sonny on the bass, Prince respected the hell out of him, and you could just tell he did. It was fairly rare that you would sense that from Prince, but with a lot of his band, he was sort of like that."

Perhaps in an effort to work outside of his traditional comfort zone of Paisley Park studios, engineer Michael Koppelman recalled that "we did basic tracks for a lot of the album's songs in London, because Prince was there for ten days playing Wembley Stadium, so we had a studio going every day, and had the band set up, and they tracked a whole bunch of stuff. We also did a bunch of the recording at Paisley, so I'd say it was roughly half and half. So the basics were done in London, Paisley, and a little bit in Japan." Another update Prince made to his recording routine—this time a technical one—during the tracking for '*Diamonds and Pearls*' was one that Koppelman recalled as "a change that I take a little credit or blame for is introducing him to Midi, because I had this little Apple mac portable that I had a sequencer on. So we were at Larrabee Sound in L.A., and I hooked it up to all the gear, just for the hell of it, and I showed it to him, 'Hey, check this out.' So he recorded some stuff, and we worked on this little groove in my computer, and it crashed and everything was lost, and we'd only fooled around for like 10 minutes, and he kind of laughed at me and left, because he was on his way out. But Midi crept back in because we used one when we were doing Ingrid Chavez's album, and pretty soon he started using it, then pretty soon he had his own computer; and within a short time after that, he was doing more and more Midi and more looping, and sampling—stuff like that. I think the main things he liked about Midi were: since we never locked to tape, we had to use audio triggers to move things around, so we would trigger the sampler with the snare to grab the backgrounds, then trigger it again to play it back to move the background, and it was just sort of a cumbersome process. So as soon as we were running Midi time codes—Simpti and beats—once we knew what our beats were, then we could do all that stuff really easy. So I think part of the selling point was: you could still manipulate the sound and you're not committing that stuff to tape. We also got beats on tape, so we could move things around really easy, cut and paste. And I think those were probably the reasons we started doing it more and more. Because he could say 'Okay, move the backgrounds, I'll be back in an hour,' and we could move the backgrounds around in Midi, and it went much quicker."

Expanding further on Prince's recording routine in the studio during this period, fellow Paisley Park engineer Sylvia Massey began by explaining that "he has a very interesting way of working which is mind-blowing, because he's so prolific he would have 3 or 4 studios going at all at the same time, and I'd be in one of the studios and he'd say 'Okay, take this tape', which was an old Revolution-era 2-inch tape, and he'd say 'Okay, make 7 copies of that song,' and then he'd have maybe four rooms all working on the same master, and he would take and erase a bass track, and play a new bass track, and then take each copy of the Revolution-era outtakes, and change it slightly—so now he'd have 7 new songs, because the bass line would be different with a few extra percussion parts, a new guitar riff…When I worked with him, this was how he worked: He would play two bars of one riff on a guitar, and he would play a drum beat live on a drum machine with one hand and the bassline on another keyboard with the other hand… He'll start adding to it. He'll lay another part down…And so I would be working on one of these copies, and then he would kick me out of the studio, and work on vocals entirely by himself. So I would have the room ready for him, have the mic hanging over the console all buzzed and on a ready track, and he would do all the engineering himself—he'd do lead vocals, doubles, backing vocals, harmonies…He never allowed me to be in the studio when he did vocals. The vocal mic was set up over the console so that he could do his own recording and comping for all vocal parts--I think he's very shy about his vocals in the studio…and four hours later, I'd be waiting outside the door, he'd call me in and say 'OK, first riff is the verses, second riff in the choruses, there's your drum beat for the whole song, put it all together…please mix it, and I'll be back.' And then leave. Then he'd go from studio to studio and do the same thing, so in one day, each studio would finish 2 songs, he was cranking out this song machine."

Continuing, Massey explained that "the thing about Prince is that he has the final product already swimming in his head; he knows what it's going to sound like. He could get it there himself--he could engineer it, he could produce it, he could perform every part himself faster than anyone else--but he prefers to have other people put it together…and who knows when he'd be back, but you'd better get on it, cause it better be ready by the time he gets back…I got really good with my skills by working with Prince, because the minute that he walks in the studio, you better be ready to record. The minute he picked up an instrument, you better be in record, and if you miss one thing, you're outta there. So I learned how to be really fast and really on the ball and really pay attention to everything that was going on in the session with Prince."

Beginning foundationally with the album's drum sound, which the *Philadelphia Daily News* complimentarily noted "features a genuine live drummer, chunkmeister Michael B., lending lots of sparks and punch to…(the) rhythm section." Engineer Michael Koppelman recalled that while "Prince almost never played drums using a click track, Michael would play with a click once in a while, but Prince never did. When I miced the drums up for D&P, we used the D-112 on the kick almost all the time, we also liked the 414s on the snare, but we also sometimes did 421s and 57s. With the toms, this company had come out with these specialized dynamic mics for recording drums." Continuing, Koppelman explained of the album's rhythm tracks—recorded in both London and back in the U.S. at Paisley Park—that "we did play in some good rooms. For instance, when we were recording in London we miced up with a lot of different pairs of room mics just to find the best ones to use. But at Paisley, in Studio A, the drum room is pretty little, so we just had a couple overheads, and had a tube C24 mic which we would sometimes use for a room mic or for overheads. It was fucking beautiful for overheads, a little bit wasteful, so I would say that was about it in our normal course of recording. In London, we had a couple of really nice sounding rooms, so we tried to get natural drum ambience, so we did sort of in the normal recording engineer dork sort of way try to get really good room mics. And I used to love putting reverb on ONLY the room mics to just to try and accent the room without putting the reverb right on the drum."

Turning from the album's basic backing tracks, which Koppelman further recalled were "usually tracked with the whole band, Prince would go out with them and they'd sort of jam and we'd record. For guitars, Prince had this really weird-shaped white guitar, and he actually did use that in the studio some. I think he was using Marshall Amps at that time, miced with a set of 87 mics. We also got some room tones with some C-24s. He would usually start out playing something with the band during basic tracking, and then do his own overdubs. There were other times where he'd play a piano or keyboard instead, and sometimes, he'd have them on the studio side, and he'd be in the control room with a keyboard, but that was less frequent." Once the New Power Generation's basic backing tracks had been laid on a given song, Koppelman explained that Prince next "would get in streaks where he just was singing, or just be working on overdubs on some songs."

When working on guitar tracks, the engineer recollected that "Prince was sort of a craftsman on the overdubs side, so we'd work on solos for a while. Really a lot of his genius is on the overdubs side, because he would basically produce the record by overdubbing. So I remember him taking time on solos, or there would be times when he'd have a guitar solo and a keyboard would be shadowing it, playing exactly the same riffs and shit like that. And it was pretty old-school back-then, where we weren't doing any computer editing on audio tracks at all, so it was just punching in and out. So when he was done, the track would be assembled on the tape machine."

Elaborating for his own part on his creative process in terms of detail re overdubbing, Prince explained that "I always spend a lot of time and energy thinking about and seeking out those little touches. Attention to detail makes the difference between a good song and a great song. And I meticulously try to put the right sound in the right place, even sounds that you would only notice if I left them out. Sometimes I hear a melody in my head, and it seems like the first color in a painting. And then you can build the rest of the song with other added sounds. You just have to try to be with that first color, like a baby yearns to come to its parents. That's why creating music is really like giving birth. Music is like the universe: The sounds are like the planets, the air and the light fitting together. When I write an arrangement, I always picture a blind person listening to the song. And I choose chords and sounds and percussion instruments which would help clarify the feel of the song to a blind person. For instance, a fat chord can conjure up a fat person, or a particular kind of color, or a particular kind of fabric or setting that I'm singing about. Also, some chords suggest a male, others a female, and some ambient sounds suggest togetherness while others suggest loneliness."

Continuing, Koppelman explained that "Prince usually recorded his guitar tracks from the control room, which was akward at times because he would basically punch himself in when he could, and if he couldn't, he'd have one of us reach over the top of the control unit and punch him in or out, so you'd be sitting there, and he'd be punching in and out, and then say 'Come here, punch in' or 'Punch out' here or there, or sometimes just nod, and then you would punch him in or out. And we'd usually do that just a few times during a session because he could usually do it himself. It was always sort of nerve-racking, because he nodded sometimes when he was playing during a take, and might sort of nod and you thought he meant to go punch him in and he didn't. I recall some tense moments with him like that where I'd punch in when he wasn't nodding for me to punch in and I thought he was. So I'd punch in the wrong place, and he was such a good musician it never mattered, we rarely deleted anything."

Exploring the recording process for some of the album's specific tracks, which *Rolling Stone Magazine* had noted were a result of "Minneapolis' resident genius…(refocusing) his attention on his first love: pop song-craft," Koppelman, beginning with the album's lead single, '*Gett Off*', recalled that "the song came out of the band jamming, where there was a long session we did and Prince was in the studio with the band and Levi and Sonny, everybody…it was around the same time we were track-ing '*Cream.*' Out of that song, we got a B-Side called '*Violet the Organ Grinder*', he took the '*Gett Off*'jam and we made like 12 or 15 songs out of it through various mixes in one day. And Sylvia Massey recorded the vocal on that, but it's one of the great off-spring that came out of '*Gett Off*'. We recorded those all in like 24 hours, where we'd copy it off onto a new tape, start banging on it and make a new song out of it in an hour or two, then make another copy, go to another song. It was non-stop."

When turning his attention to another of the album's hit singles—'*Money Don't Matter Tonite*', a song that *Entertainment Weekly* excitedly noted was "sung in a soulful growl that sounds utterly unaffected, and it sports a slinky, subtle groove that recalls the maturity of Stevie Wonder's early-'70s heyday," engineer Michael Koppelman recalled of recording the album's vocal collaboration between Prince and back-up vocalist Rosie Gaines that "I remember Prince was recording vocals for the song, and I had set him up with the mic, and he said 'Test, test, test… Louder,' so I turned up the pre, then he went 'Test, test, test, okay see ya', so I left and came back and the needle was just fucking buried the whole time through on his vocal track. And when I pointed out to him that he'd buried it the whole way through, but then I said 'I kind of like it,' and he was like 'Yeah, I kind of like it too,' so we just left it. But that vocal, you can tell it's fried, on the vinyl record it's fried." Elaborating further on the song's creation, Rosie Gaines further recollected that "I sang the melody to Prince and he immediately wanted to put a demo down. So I was up all night, all the next day."

Of the creation of '*Cream*,' arguably the album's biggest-performing hit single, which the Philadelphia Inquirer noted "seems tailor-made for hip-grinding on the dance floor (or anywhere else you dare)," and which reached # 1 on the Billboard Pop Singles Chart, engineer Michael Koppelman explained that "it was one that Prince had fully formed in his head when he walked in the room. I recall that it was a song that went down to tape very fast, and you can tell there's a lot of fine detail in the production, so Prince did take his time on the overdubs and such right. Prince and Levi and Michael tracked the rhythm track. We had really good room sounds on the drums. We recorded it at Studio A at Paisley, and I'd say it was probably 95% done by the end of the first day of recording on the song. We worked on over-dubs probably a couple of mornings after that, and it was done. We had mixed '*Cream*' before we gave it to Keith, the mix engineer on the song, and I thought we had it pretty close, but he was the person who sort of really hypes up the mix, tons of upper-mids, and really in your face, and that was kind of his style at the time."

Delving into the recording process for some of the album's non-single tracks, Koppelman recalled that, for as much work as the album's hit singles received right up to the album's release, "there are other songs on that record we never touched, including '*Willing and Able*,' where there was basically a rough mix that I had done when we first cut it into the sketch-up, and we never touched it again." Still, the latter was rarely the case, with the engineer further recalling that "*Live for Love*,' we had a done mix of that song sitting in the can, and he came in one day and had totally re-written the lyrics. I remember I'd mixed that song and thought it was fucking awesome and I was really happy with it, and then we never used it because he totally re-sang it. He came in one day during the Iraq thing, and said 'How can I let a song out that is sort of glorifying war when this is going on and people's kids are dying out there? I can't release that song,' he actually said that, and then went and changed the WHOLE song."

When principle tracking for the album was completed and attention turned to its mixing, engineer Michael Koppelman began by outlining the sonic goal "in mixing for Prince, that I was mainly just trying to take things out and strip things down, and I tell a story that I once put up the tape for the song '*Sign O'the Times*', and there's like 6 tracks, there's nothing on that tape, and it's awesome. And I was hoping to get Prince into that more minimalist vibe, that's where I was hoping to push him and he was going exactly the opposite way. I hate the 'Wall of Sound' sort of approach, and Prince in those days was using tons and tons and tons of tracks. With some of the songs on 'Diamonds and Pearls', we had 2 24-tracks hooked up, and sometimes one of those was a bounce from another machine. Things were out of hand, and Prince was just experimenting—on the good side, he'd go 'Screw it, I want to fool around with a different bass or a different drum loop,' so we'd end up building a song on top of a song. You never really knew what he was going to leave in and what he was going to leave out, so for me, mixing was a process of 'What can I take out, and how much can I take out?' So Prince and I had kind of a tension there, in that I would be trying to take everything out, and I remember him joking with me once after listening to one of my mixes, 'Can I put my song back now?' And he unmuted all the stuff I had muted. I was also into the Cocteau Twins and stuff like that back then, so I was into heavier effects, reverbs and stuff' so for instance, the song '*Diamonds and Pearls*' I mixed, and Prince came in and grabbed every fader that had a return from effects and turned them all down 10 DB each, and that song is still just ridiculously wet when I listen to it today, it cracks me up."

When he and Prince turned their focus to mixing the album's powerful stacks of vocal tracks, Koppelman recalled that, at that time, "the direction in general was huge and in your face. Prince was listening to that '*Everybody Dance Now*' hit and rap stuff, and he'd play some of it in the studio and it was HUGE, in your face loud stuff. That's what Prince was on about in that era, was being big, fat and loud with his sound. So that's the direction he gave us. Specifically with me and mixing vocals, the DVX compressors have this 'over easy' mode, and I would just squish the living fuck out of Prince's voice with the DVX over easy compression, and taking 10, 15, 20 DBs out, because the overhidians were really super-fast, luxorheads, so I would literally squish the living fuck out of it. Same with the SSL compressor in the board, the 2-mix compressor, Prince and I had a mutual interest in just seeing how hard you could hit the compressor, and how hard you hit the tumba. We both go through different stages, I remember stages where we'd have the needles tagged, because he saw some engineer doing that he thought that was how you made it sound loud. Then we'd go the other way where we left tons of headroom where we'd wack it way into the compressor or just barely, we were experimenting with that sort of shit. I remember one day I came in and he was like 'Hey, come here, check this out!' And he was pointing at the Tumba and the meters are barely moving, like there's all sorts of headroom, and he's like 'Check it out!' It was sort of funny."

Rolling Stone Magazine in their stellar review of Prince's commercial come-back LP proclaimed that "PRINCE HAS NEVER SOUNDED SANER than he does on *Diamonds and Pearls,*" further reporting that, on October 1st, 1991, Prince "released his fifth album in five years, *Diamonds and Pearls* (Number Three, 1991), which spawned Top Ten hits in the lascivious '*Gett Off*' (Number 21, 1991), '*Cream*' (Number One, 1991), and the title track (Number three, 1992). Warner Bros. made Prince a vice president when he re-signed with the label in 1992." For critics, the record universally seemed to mark a return for Prince to his former chart-topping musical glory, with the Detroit Free Press hailing the album as "a pleasant and at times inspiring listen. And it sounds like the beginning of a new period for Prince that has potential for artistic, as well as commercial, advancement...Prince has made a welcome and refreshing return to popcraft." The New Musical Express, for its part, concluded the new record represented " Prince...reborn," while *Entertainment Weekly* seemed to feel the Minneapolis Genius's latest musical offering was a successful acknowledgement of the fact that "Prince seems to realize there's a lot riding on his new album, *Diamonds and Pearls.*" Selling over 6 million copies worldwide, and four million in the U.S. alone, the record was Prince's clear signal to the world over that he was back, inspiring many of the aforementioned critics, including the Detroit Free Press, to conclude Prince had struck "gold with his new album…thanks to a handful of ace tracks, '*Diamonds and Pearls*'…may march Prince back into the hit parade."

> *"He is an artist capable of altering popular consciousness in concrete ways."*
>
> —*Rolling Stone Magazine*

"Prince's latest album is quite easily one of the most exciting to be released this year—an excellent funk collection, a dance-floor stomper and an essential disc in any self-respecting music lover's collection."

—St. Paul Pioneer Press

Chapter 22:

The LoveSymbol LP—1993

Prince's fourteenth studio LP, the *LoveSymbol LP*, was released on October 13th, 1992, merely a year after the smash success of *'Diamonds & Pearls.'* Hailed as usual by *Rolling Stone Magazine* as sounding "funkier than he's been in ages," while *Entertainment Weekly* praised Prince's newest studio offering as "irrepressibly catchy," and *Billboard Magazine* concluded that *"the Love Symbol Album* has some of the finest, most inventive music of Prince's career." Part of that credit—according to the same publication—came from Prince's choice to forgo the one-man band route for the band he debuted on *Diamonds & Pearls* w/the New Power Generation, which Billboard hailed for fulfilling "their potential on *The Love Symbol Album*...(which) sounds like a band performing together, working off of each other's strengths." *Entertainment Weekly*, for its part, had equal praise for Prince's "dazzling current band, the New Power Generation, can deliver styles far removed from rock and funk (though it's far more impressive playing jazz, with rambunctious solo snippets on trombone and baritone sax)."

According to primary album engineer Dave Friedlander, "the *LoveSymbol LP* was more a band session, and it was interesting to see him go from when I first started working them primarily playing a lot of the instruments himself to actually finding the band with Morris, Tommy and Michael—and trusting them enough to let them play the song. So he'd call the band and say 'I wrote some songs last night, come on in, we're gonna record them,' and he'd teach each band member the parts they were going to play. When he did that he was patient, but was very, very, very specific about the parts he wanted played. So it wasn't like 'Hey, play something like this,' it was 'Play this.' They were great about picking it up, and it was an amazing thing to watch: this vision come together in a matter of 20 minutes, half an hour from people never hearing the song to having this full-on performance. There were no rehearsals either, Prince would show the band the parts and they would dive right in. Typically, I would get a call and he'd say 'Set up the band how we like to set up the band,' meaning don't sway from the standard that we've established. And that standard—for the *LoveSymbol* LP—was everyone in the same room except for percussion."

Elaborating on Prince's studio set-up preferences during the recording of the LP, Friedlander recalled that "what I did at Paisley was pretty much standard for everything I worked on as far as specific instrumentation, that stuff didn't really change. The thing about Prince was: when he found something he liked, he didn't want to experiment a lot in the recording process. So if he found a drum sound he liked, the next time he tracked drums and you went to get a drum sound, you'd have to use the same microphones and put the drums in the exact same place. So the frustrating thing was not having the time or the option to be creative with your micing techniques from session to session." The latter insistence, according to the engineer, was primarily due to the simple fact that "for Prince, he was getting his ideas down as quickly as possible before new songs came, so he was not one to sit around and wait, he wanted to create. And we're not just talking about one song in his head, it could be any number of songs. For me, working for Prince was the hardest thing I've ever done, and at the same time, the most rewarding. He was a hard cat to work for simply because he demanded perfection, and he wanted things done with speed and authenticity, and he just wanted people surrounding him that could keep up with his pace. It was intense, because you had to be sharp after 48 hours of no sleep, but he didn't sleep. He would go home for an hour to take a bath and change clothes, and I think that was his 'sleep.' "

For the album's drum tracking, Friedlander explained that "I would use an AKG-112 on the kick drum, I don't believe I used an undersnare mic, and for the snare, we had gotten some Yamaha mics that were just the shit that we used on the snare and toms. They were snare-specific, and the plug for the mic cable came out of the bottom of the microphone—so it was at a 90 degree angle to the microphone—and that was the identifying feature to those microphones. They just appeared one day, and there was a smaller one for the snare, and then three others for the toms. For overheads, I was really into the Crown PZMs because of their phase coherency and the full, stereo sound, so whenever I would mic up the drums, I'd use the Crowns for overheads. You can either put the PZMs back to back against each other, or hang them with some type of barrier between them. The bigger the barrier the more separation you get between the left and right mics, so I would tape the PZM mics to different sides of a clipboard, and hang it over the drums. Because the tassles are so close together, you get a really good phase response, and also they just sounded really brilliant on the symbols. That was my standard go-to there."

When attention turned to a Tower-of-Power equivalent horns section that the San Jose Mercury News hailed for its "blues horns and a swing jazz punch and traces of the boiling funk of George Clinton," engineer Dave Friedlander began by explaining that "I had been on a hiatus from Paisley at the start of the LoveSymbol LP, and was called back because—prior to Prince's horns recording for 'Sexy MF'—I had recorded George Clinton's horn section in the stone room. George's horn section had consisted of all the standard characters—Eric Leeds playing sax, Macio and Fred Westley from James Brown's band. It was like the horn section to die for. So long story short, I took my leave of absence and Prince pulled back in to do 'Sexy MF', and the first thing he said when I got back was 'So you recorded the horns for George, right?' And I said, 'Yes,' and he said 'Can you record my horns like that?' And I said 'I don't know Man, that's the horny horns!' And I thought he was going to be cocky, but he said 'You're right,' and acknowledging that, he next said 'But you can make my horn section sound like that?' "

Delving into the specifics of how he sonically accomplished just that with Prince's *NPG Hornheadz*—consisting of — Friedlander continued, recalling that "Studio A had this amazing room that had this imported Italian marble in it, like a stone room, which sounded really bright, and then also had a smaller isolation room as well. In the marble room, I always liked to record horns in there. So I set them up the same way, with a U-47 on the Berry Sax, and for the trumpet, I usually used a 414 or something with a smaller diaphragm like a AKG 460, definitely one of those, which changed depending on the song. If there was a trombone player, we always had an AKG D-12, and for Saxaphones, I normally used Neumanns, like a 47 and also a C-12. I usually tried to use whatever tube mics we had kicking around, and the mics were arranged in a semi-circle, and I would then also have a couple of mics in the center of them—in a X-Y (where the microphones are crossed at 90 degrees, so one mic is shooting toward the trumpet, and the other toward the Berry Sax), and to pick up more room on the Sexy MF sessions, I put the a set of 414s in a figure-8 pattern, instead of being cardioid. That was pretty standard to try and capture the room. I would normally do the figure-8 pattern if I was in Studio A where there was a bit more volume to the room, which is called the Blumlein pattern."

Once he had the band set-up for recording on what he referred to as the '*Sexy M.F.*' session, Friedlander recalled that—not surprisingly given the company they were playing in w/Prince—"those horn sections went really quick, and the players were so amazing—beyond studio musicians—because the odd thing was nobody there really read music—they weren't readers. Like Prince, they for the most part played by ear. So within a half-hour of starting learning the tune, it was on tape. To me, that blew my mind, because if you think about the subtleties of performance, it seems like it would take a lot longer than a half hour to learn an arrangement. But these guys not only learned the song without charting it out, but were also able to put such feeling and emotion into it as well. Not just mechanically playing it through, but really making it groove, and dynamically go up and down, so for not being readers, it was amazing to watch. We hammered out most of the album's horn parts in that one-day session, and when Prince showed the band their parts, he knew exactly what he wanted, specifically, but he still gave the players a lot of respect and freedom in how they performed those parts. But he definitely had specifics for dynamics and for how phrases were to go, volumes, and tightness, so he had really specific ideas of exactly how the parts should go, and knew exactly when a given take was the keeper take."

While his band was out in the main room of Studio A, Friedlander recalled that —for the recording of Prince's own instrumental and vocal parts—as usual, "The control room was the heart of Prince's whole operation—when he wasn't playing a drum kit, that's where everything was performed. Everything was back behind the console—from keyboards to guitars—it was all set up right there so he didn't have to move 2 inches to get any instrument—everything was always set up and ready to go. That's the reason we had to upgrade the console in Studio A, because he pretty much had every instrument you would want to record ready to go at any given instance. And for that type of thing, you need a lot of real estate on a board. So he'd have two 24-track machines locked up for a 48-track mix, well you need 48 channels just for the console returns from the tape machine. Then you've got a drum kit and drum machine set-up, and maybe 8 different keyboard modules set up, and a bass set-up, and a guitar-set-up, so that's like 24 to 32 channels worth of inputs. And we haven't even talked about effects returns for your mix then as well. So he had that new SSL brought in with 2 wings on it, and 96 inputs on it, which was just heaven-sent, because it just made things a whole lot easier. So you could dedicate a bank of 24 channels to instruments, and just have them there and ready, which made things a lot easier."

Once Prince began recording vocals and guitar tracks for the *LoveSymbol LP*, Friedlander began by explaining that for the album's acoustic guitars—such as those heard on the smash single '*Seven*'—"we had those Stephen Paul-modified AKG-C12s mics, we had two of them, which were cream. We even traveled with the C-12s, because being modified, the capsules were shaved down, and those things were just bright and gorgeous. I've never heard a C-12 like them. So when he did his acoustic guitar tracks, he wouldn't kick us out of the room, we'd all put head-phones on, and he would pull the C-12 down from the vocal position and we'd mic up his acoustic right there behind the board, between the sound hole and the bottom of the neck of the guitar. For his electric guitars, with Prince being the baddest ass guitar player in the world in my opinion, his guitar rig was constantly changing, as were guitars—he had so many guitars you could only imagine. At the time, he was getting these guitars that were made by some violin maker in Germany that resembled the white guitar from Purple Rain. So I never saw him play many standard off-the-shelf guitars, they were all these custom made guitars. I miced his rig with a 57 straight up on the cone, and a D-12 at like a 45 degree angle to that microphone, so they were both pointed at the same speaker cone. He had these 412 cabinets, but we would only mic one speaker, and then I would stick a C-12 out in the room if he wanted any room sound, and those all went through these SSL G-series mic pre's, and combining the two mics at the console. As far as guitar effects, he had this weird Roland box where a lot of the delay, chorus, pitch-bendy effects all came from. He had a huge pedal board in the control room that had everything on it. He used the C-12 primarily for his vocals as well, which he usually recorded alone."

When Prince turned attention to tracking the album's keyboards and related programming—be it rhythm tracks or sampling—Friedlander explained that "the Roland D-50 was his mainstay as far as keyboards went. He was a pre-set kind of dude, he wasn't really a programmer, so he would just find a pre-set that did what he wanted to do, and would experiment with different sounds until he found something he liked. He also used the Akia S1000 sampler for drum sampling during that record too, we had a whole library of drum sounds to choose from if he wanted. The LM1 was also around during that record—and I've never seen anyone play a drum machine like Prince did in my life, it was a performance, because he would stop the machine mid-song, do a fill with his fingers on the pad, then start the machine back up, and even though there was only one pattern running, but if you listen to it it doesn't sound like it. He had the mix-output of the drum machine running into a bunch of foot pedals that were mounted right above the drum machine, so he's hitting these delay and flange pedals and just tweaking the fuck out of the drum machine. It was so cool, because he could take one pattern and make it into this insane performance. Part of that was having the song in his head so he knew where the drum fills go, because most people couldn't play the drums till the song was down, but Prince could do this drum performance with all the breaks and everything spot-on with no other music going. It was a trip to watch." Of Prince's longtime studio mainstay sampler—the Publison—Friedlander, who had begun working with Prince in 1988, quipped that, by 1992, "the Publison was the bane of all of our existence. It was this multi-effects box, and pretty unique in that it allowed you to sample something and play it back via your keyboard, so you could play a sample you'd taken up and down the keyboard and it would change the pitch of the sample, but wouldn't change the length of the sample. With any normal sampler, as you go up the keyboard, sure the pitch is going to rise, but the speed of it is also going to go faster as well, just like a record. So the Publison was the first unit that actually allowed you to change the pitch without changing the length of time. So if you wanted to create a harmony to a part, you could do it instantly, change the pitch, and the time would be exactly the same. So when he would want to do a guitar part and wanting it up an octave like some of his weird high guitar parts, we could either slow the tape down to half-speed, or sample it in the Publison and fly it in an octave higher, and it would be the same time. That's why he really liked to use it, so he could sample vocals and just flying stuff around, sampling Clare Fisher's string parts for one song and using a little piece of it for another song. So that was Prince's main go-to sampler, and I wouldn't be surprised if Prince isn't still using it."

When he'd completed principle tracking and turned to mixing, Friedlander began by revealing that "for the most part, Prince was really nice to give us all this really great credit on his recordings, but to be honest with you, a lot of times, we were just glorified assistants. He knows how to record and mix, he could do everything behind the board. We were next to him, but he was in control, not like a typical recording session where the engineer would be sitting behind the console and the artist would be on the couch. Prince was full-on hands-on, so as an engineer assisting him, you had to know your shit. When we worked on a mix with Prince, we'd set it up and then he'd come in and dial it back to his taste, and take the helm after we were done, as you'd expect a producer to do. He would just sit down and make adjustments. In terms of vocal effects Prince liked to use when mixing, definitely we had a Lexicon 480 reverb hanging around, that was our standard reverb, and we'd typically have that reverb and a delay always set up, and we'd use a Eventide H3000 quite a bit as kind of a stereo program, where we'd tune the left side down a little bit pitch-wise, and the right side we'd tune up a little bit pitch-wise, and put a little delay on the left side on the left and right sides, so when you turned it on, it took the mono sound and spread it out and made it sound pretty big in stereo, and so we used that a lot on background vocals just to widen them and spread them out. So while we were mixing, he'd maybe let us start a mix—and on a couple of occasions, actually let us mix a couple things—but for the most part, Prince is an engineer."

Upon release, the LoveSymbol LP, which debuted at # 5 on Billboard's Top 200 Album Chart, was hailed by *Billboard Magazine* as featuring "Prince's best dance tracks since the Black Album… But Prince wasn't content; he decided to run the gamut of modern pop/R&B/dance, and the music is uniformly accomplished and excellent," while *Billboard Magazine* concluded that the album "recalls the glory days of James Brown and the JB's...rarely has his protean musicality been more pleasurable." Producing the hit singles 'Sexy M.F.' (# 4 UK), 'My Name is Prince' (# 7 UK), and 'Seven' (# 7 US), Spin Magazine ranked the album as one of the '20 Best Albums Of The Year,' while the Village Voice's ranking had Prince's latest offering as the 14th best album of the year's Top 40 LPs. *Entertainment Weekly*, in an A rated review of the LP, hailed Prince on his new album as "funky, funkier than ever before, maybe even the funkiest musician around right now… Just about all the music on the album is irrepressibly catchy, and also impressively complicated: Prince brings a whole musical city to life," while NME Magazine complimented "Prince's musical vision is positively hallucinogenic." The album's greatest notes of critical praise came from Prince's hometown papers, beginning with the Minneapolis Star-Tribune 's declaration that "admirably, Prince evokes Ellington" on the new LP, while the St. Paul Pioneer Press—giving Prince arguably his best compliment in years—concluded that "this is an album Michael Jackson can only hope to make…Prince's latest album is quite easily one of the most exciting to be released this year—an excellent funk collection, a dance-floor stomper and an essential disc in any self-respecting music lover's collection."

"His discipline is one of his greatest assets...He's always aware of how much talent there is out there and how good he has to be to be competitive."

—Prince's Longtime 80s
Studio Engineer Susan Rogers

Conclusion:

1992 and Beyond...

With the *LoveSymbol* album, released on October 13th, 1992, debuting at # 5 on the Billboard Top 200 Chart, producing the hit singles '*Sexy M.F.*' (# 4, UK), '*My Name is Prince*' (#36 US, #7 UK), and the record's biggest smash, '*7*' (#7 US), Prince would produce a masterpiece that *Billboard Magazine* noted "has Prince's best dance tracks since *The Black Album*. But Prince wasn't content; he decided to run the gamut of modern pop/R&B/dance, and the music is uniformly accomplished and excellent...*The Love Symbol Album* has some of the finest, most inventive music of Prince's career."

That career would take some predictably unpredictable twists and turns over the next decade, beginning with the 1994 release of '*The Most Beautiful Girl in the World,*', which reached # 1 on the Billboard Top 200 Album Chart, and marking Prince's first release under the newly-introduced professional moniker of an unpronounceable symbol, which many thought would be the death of his commercial career. Still, it was *Billboard Magazine/All Music Guide* who would point out that the song "became his biggest hit in years," and thereafter inspire *Rolling Stone Magazine* to determine in their review of 1995's '*The Gold Experience*— which was released on September 26th, 1995, and produced the hits 'P. Control' and 'I Hate U' (# 11, US)—that with "this LP, our former Prince turns in his most effortlessly eclectic set since 1987's *Sign o' the Times... The Gold Experience* is surprisingly retro in sound and attitude. Longtime fans will recognize signature riffs from *Purple Rain, 1999* and *Controversy,* as well as customized appropriations from glitter rock, the Ohio Players, art rock and the kind of quirky narrative poems Prince perfected upon the release of *Graffiti Bridge*...What you really hear is the heart, soul and mind of our once and future Prince."

The full measure of Prince's recorded genius will take generations to comprehensively absorb, in part because, as the artist has revealed, "I've got a thousand songs in the vaults, finished songs... I could probably release five to seven albums every year if I wanted to-polished stuff that I'm really happy with." If not for the simple fact that it would take that long to issue all of the unreleased material hibernating in his vault, equally as time-consuming, *Time Magazine* wisely points out, would be the fact that "musicians and producers are likely to pour over...(his records), scratching their heads and wondering how he does it." Aware of how far he has traveled in pop music already—light years past even his closest comparable peers—Prince recently reasoned that, for now at least, "I have it pretty well mastered. I'm always learning, though. I like to believe that it's infinite, too, so once one can do whatever it is that one desires with any one particular art form, then I would suppose they would have mastered it. So in that case, to answer your question, then yes." Still, the artist appears hardly finished, arguing in the same time that while "you can't push the envelope any further than I pushed it... There's no more envelope to push. I pushed it off the table. It's on the floor. Let's move forward now."

With well over 1000 unreleased songs in his infamous 'vault', which sits under 24-hour-a-day armed guard, we may never know the full depths of Prince's musical brilliance till well into the next century, with the singer himself acknowledging that "I have everything on tape, man, including all the informal jams. I record everything I do, just like Jimi Hendrix did. And eventually a lot of it will be released." It prompted the Rock & Roll Hall of Fame to observe that "given such prolific output, it doesn't take long to realize that Prince isn't just a musician but a force of nature." For her own part, longtime engineer Susan Rogers, who recorded MUCH of the unreleased material hibernating in Prince's vault, feels that ultimately, he owes it to both his own genius and the love from his fans to in time "release all of his songs in their original form. I think he is an important figure in American music and with that comes (somewhat of) a responsibility to provide a record of his artistic progress. Artistic license means he can release whatever he wants of his own intellectual property but I think that when a true genius comes along, society benefits from seeing what he or she produced. It is understandable that he wouldn't release them today, but I hope they are packaged so that someday those old recordings are available to the public."

The legacy Prince has already left is just a beginning to understanding his longer-term impact on pop music derivatively-speaking as that influence continues to unfold in the next generation of Prince-shaped Pop. In this time, he's off to a head start, having already been ranked by *Rolling Stone Magazine* as #28 on their list of the 100 Greatest Artists of All Time, praised therein for the fact that "(no other) artist has swung as fluently from style to style (hard rock, stripped-down funk, jazzy show tunes, intoxicated balladry, kid-pop, dance raunch), and only JB has put on more incendiary live shows. And if Prince had done nothing but stand stock still onstage and sung other people's material, he'd have locked up his place in the Rock and Roll Hall of Fame; in the last three decades, popular music has produced few finer singers…As a guitarist, with Hendrix and Steve Cropper; (and as a songwriter), he ranks with Lennon and McCartney, Bob Dylan, and Smokey Robinson."

Billboard Magazine, elaborating on the breadth of Prince's influence over modern mainstream pop music, likewise credited him as "one of the most singular talents of the rock & roll era, capable of seamlessly tying together pop, funk, folk, and rock. Not only did he release a series of groundbreaking albums; he toured frequently, produced albums and wrote songs for many other artists, and recorded hundreds of songs that still lie unreleased in his vaults. With each album he released, Prince has shown remarkable stylistic growth and musical diversity, constantly experimenting with different sounds, textures, and genres...no other contemporary artist can blend so many diverse styles into a cohesive whole."

With his 2004 induction into the Rock & Roll Hall of Fame, Prince's legend is best summed up in the Hall's conclusion that with his singular sound, Prince "rewrote the rulebook, forging a synthesis of black funk and white rock that served as a blueprint for cutting-edge music in the Eighties. Prince made dance music that rocked and rock music that had a bristling, funky backbone...(His) revolutionary music made Prince a figure comparable in paradigm-shifting impact to Little Richard, James Brown, Jimi Hendrix and George Clinton...(In 2003), an album of lengthy, jazz-funk instrumentals, garnered a Grammy nomination for the ever-resourceful artist known formerly and forever as Prince...(proving) Prince is never uninteresting and always capable one more hit record or a return to stardom."

Showing no signs of slowing down with a slew of new albums released in recent years, including 2004's 3x platinum *'Musicology'* LP, which hit # 1 on the Billboard Top 200 Album Chart, won 2 Grammy Awards, and produced the hit single *'Musicology'* (#3 US), 2006's *'3121'*, which also debuted at # 1 atop Billboard's Top 200 album chart, producing the hit singles *'Black Sweat'* and *'Fury,'* 2007's *'Planet Earth,'* which debuted at # 3 on Billboard's Top 200 album chart, producing the hit single *'Guitar,'* and 2009's *'LotusFlower'*, which marked the 25th studio album released by Prince in his 30+ year recording career. Debuting at # 2 on the Billboard Top 200 album chart, the album inspired *Rolling Stone Magazine* to hail the 3-CD set, not surprisingly, as "brilliant."

When asked about his future musical plans given his recent commercial resurgence, Prince reasons in answering that "there has always been a dichotomy in my music...I'm searching for a higher plane, but I want the most of being on earth...It's hard for me to answer that because I am music...People are calling this my comeback. Comeback? I never went anywhere...I never stopped playing and recording. Never had a problem filling arenas...It's me—I'm just doing what I always do and what I love to do. But someone has to do this, because no one else is. The music is such a treasure, so celebratory and joyous, and no one's doing it anymore—I'm happy to keep it going."

About the Author

Nashville-based music biographer **Jake Brown** has written twenty published books, including *Heart: in the Studio, Prince: in the Studio, Rick Rubin: in the Studio, Dr. Dre: In the Studio*; *Suge Knight: The Rise, Fall and Rise of Death Row Records*; *50 Cent: No Holds Barred*; *Biggie Smalls: Ready to Die*; *Tupac: In the Studio* (authorized by the estate); as well as titles on Kanye West, R. Kelly, Jay Z, the Black Eyed Peas, and non-hip hop titles including *Red Hot Chili Peppers: In the Studio, Motley Crue: In the Studio, 'Alice in Chains: in the Studio'* and the *Behind the Boards* Rock Producers Anthology Series.

Brown was also a contributing author in Rick James' recently published autobiography, *Memoirs of Rick James: Confessions of a Super Freak*, and in February 2008, appeared as the official biographer of record on Fuse TV's *Live Through This: Nikki Sixx* TV special. He has received additional coverage/press in national publications including: USA TODAY, MTV. com, *Vibe, Publishers Weekly*, etc.

Brown is also owner of the hard rock label Versailles Records, distributed nationally by Big Daddy Music/MVD Distribution. The company is celebrating its 10th anniversary in business this year.

ORDER FORM

WWW.AMBERBOOKS.COM

Fax Orders: 480-283-0991
Telephone Orders: 602-742-7211
Postal Orders: Send Checks & Money Orders to:
     Amber Communications Group, Inc.
     1334 E. Chandler Blvd., Suite 5-D67, Phoenix, AZ 85048
Online Orders: E-mail: Amberbk@aol.com

_____*Prince: In the Studio: 1975-1995*, ISBN #: 978-0-9790976-6-9, $16.95
_____*Red Hot Chili Peppers: In the Studio*, ISBN #: 978-0-9790976-5-2, $16.95
_____*Black Eyed Peas: Unauthorized Biography*, ISBN 978-0-9790976-4-5, $16.95
_____*Dr. Dre In the Studio*, ISBN#: 0-9767735-5-4, $16.95
_____*Kanye West in the Studio*, ISBN #: 0-9767735-6-2, $16.95
_____*Tupac Shakur—(2Pac) In the Studio*, ISBN#: 0-9767735-0-3, $16.95
_____*Jay-Z…and the Roc-A-Fella Dynasty*, ISBN#: 0-9749779-1-8, $16.95
_____*Your Body's Calling Me: The Life & Times of "Robert" R. Kelly*, ISBN#: 0-9727519-5-52, $16.95
_____*Ready to Die: Notorious B.I.G.*, ISBN#: 0-9749779-3-4, $16.95
_____*Suge Knight: The Rise, Fall, and Rise of Death Row Records*, ISBN#: 0-9702224-7-5, $21.95
_____*50 Cent: No Holds Barred*, ISBN#. 0-9767735-2-X, $16.95
_____*Aaliyah—An R&B Princess in Words and Pictures*, ISBN#: 0-9702224-3-2, $10.95
_____*You Forgot About Dre: Dr. Dre & Eminem*, ISBN#: 0-9702224-9-1, $10.95
_____*Divas of the New Millenium*, ISBN#: 0-9749779-6-9, $16.95
_____*Michael Jackson: The King of Pop*, ISBN#: 0-9749779-0-X, $29.95
_____*Rise of New Kids on the Block*, ISBN#: 978-0-9790976-7-6, $15.00

Name:_____

Company Name: _____

Address:_____

City:_____State: _____Zip:_____

Telephone: (_____)_____E-mail:_____

For Bulk Rates Call: 602-743-7211   ORDER NOW

Prince	$16.95	
Red Hot Chili Peppers	$16.95	❏ Check ❏ Money Order ❏ Cashiers Check
Black Eyed Peas	$16.95	❏ Credit Card: ❏ MC ❏ Visa ❏ Amex ❏ Discover
Dr. Dre In the Studio	$16.95	
Kanye West	$16.95	CC#_____
Tupac Shakur	$16.95	
Jay-Z…	$16.95	Expiration Date:_____
Your Body's Calling Me:	$16.95	
Ready to Die: Notorious B.I.G.,	$16.95	**Payable to:**
Suge Knight:	$21.95	Amber Communications Group, Inc.
50 Cent: No Holds Barred,	$16.95	1334 E. Chandler Blvd., Suite 5-D67
Aaliyah—An R&B Princess	$10.95	Phoenix, AZ 85048
Dr. Dre & Eminem	$10.95	**Shipping:** $5.00 per book. Allow 7 days for delivery.
Divas of the New Millenium,	$16.95	**Sales Tax:** Add 7.05% to books shipped to Arizona addresses.
Michael Jackson	$29.95	
New Kids on the Block	$16.95	**Total enclosed: $**_____

JUL -- 2016